CRIMES
AGAINST WOMEN

CRIMES AGAINST WOMEN

THREE TRAGEDIES AND THE CALL FOR REFORM IN INDIA

◆

Krishna Pokharel, Paul Beckett
and the staff of *The Wall Street Journal*

THE WALL STREET JOURNAL.

HARPER

FIRST EDITION

CURRENT AFFAIRS

Print Book Edition JUNE 2013 ISBN: 9780062312174

13 14 15 16 17 ov 10 9 8 7 6 5 4 3 2 1

Printed and bound at Thomson Press (India) Ltd.

Contents

CONTENTS

PART III: The Delhi Bus Rape

Preface

As 2012 came to a close, news of the gang rape of a young woman on a bus in India's capital generated headlines around the world. The December 16 assault on her by men wielding a metal rod, and her death two weeks later from her injuries, challenged the image of modern India as a liberal aspiring superpower of confident young professionals and benign spirituality.

Instead, it focused attention on one of the dark sides of the world's largest democracy: the struggle that many Indian women face in a country where chauvinistic and misogynistic attitudes prevail despite years of rapid economic growth.

The assault, on a woman who was putting herself through college by working shifts in a call center, laid bare a troubling dynamic: Indian women are pursuing opportunities opened up by education and the economic boom, but a deep-rooted patriarchy means society and its institutions often fail them.

The Wall Street Journal's India bureau explored the plight of India's women in great detail in the past 12 months. The three stories in this print book show how the social blight evident in the Delhi rape is a phenomenon across the country, in various forms. What the crimes chronicled here have in common is the failure of society in general, and government institutions in particular, to protect women in vulnerable situations. It is not primarily a question of inadequate laws but of incompetence or venality in their enforcement.

The result is a breakdown in the social compact that is fundamental to the idea of a modern democracy: the equal treatment of its citizens and the right of all individuals to protection under the law and by their government when danger threatens.

Instead, as these stories show, the world's largest democracy is rife with lawlessness, lacks a safety net to protect its most vulnerable citizens, and frequently shows a blatant disregard, punctuated with flashes of abject brutality, for half its population.

It is a fact of Indian life that is rarely delved into amid the trumpeting of India's economic success story or of its continued struggle to eradicate poverty. But it is a blight that, unchecked, will have just as much influence on India's future.

The *WSJ*'s reporting on these issues began with the story of a Catholic nun murdered in rural India as she tried to preserve ancient tribal ways in the face of mining expansion. In her work, Sister Valsa John Malamel faced off against villagers who wanted to reap economic benefits from local mining. She also came to the aid of a woman who had allegedly been raped but whose complaint to the police was not being taken seriously. It may have been a combination of these two separate dynamics, and the threats they posed to local men, that set the stage for a nighttime mob attack that took her life, police contend.

A few months later, the *WSJ* published an in-depth account of a young woman, Munni Khatoon, from rural Bihar, who was duped into moving to Delhi, where she was forced to marry or go into prostitution—and the disaster for her and her family that ensued. The plight of one of her daughters, dubbed "Baby Falak," was national news. The *WSJ* offered a unique reconstruction of the broader human tragedy.

What Ms. Khatoon and her children's ordeal revealed was an underbelly of exploitation of women in the heart of India's capital—and the failure of social services to identify and intervene with children at risk. India has laws that are designed to provide a safety net, even at the village level, for children in need of protection, and the social welfare minister in the family's home state of Bihar acknowledged that little Falak's predicament could have been prevented had those laws been effectively enforced.

But combating human trafficking is not a high priority, and, the minister added, "The general public is not even bothered about it." Nor was it bothered about a young woman who was seeking to escape an abusive husband, the father of her kids—until after tragedy had struck.

Less than a year after Baby Falak's story gripped the nation, a young woman was on her way home from watching *Life of Pi* with a male friend when they boarded a bus toward her home. What happened next is the stuff of nightmares: five men and a teenager—the only other people on the bus—turned on the couple, beat them, sexually assaulted her, and threw them both out, naked, on the side of a highway. The bus, its inside lights turned off and the victims' appeals for help unheard or ignored, plied some of the capital's major thoroughfares for almost an hour unchecked.

Later, when demonstrators took the streets to protest what had happened, and the lack of women's safety in India in general, they were met with volleys from water cannons and charges by police wielding bamboo truncheons.

The *WSJ* led global coverage of the crime. It published intimate portraits of the victim and her friend, who tried to save her but couldn't. It delved into the lives of their alleged assailants and their communities and backgrounds. And it looked more broadly at the culture of harassment that Indian women face, which sometimes flares into violent crime.

In this print book, we bring together these stories, updated with fresh details of the individuals' lives, to show the hopes and the catastrophes, the bravery and the abuse, that are the daily lot of millions of India's women. We hope that it will prove insightful reading and provide a meticulously detailed, accurately reported, sensitively told reference point for one of the biggest issues facing one of the world's most fascinating, and important, countries.

PART I

The Murder of Sister Valsa

A WSJ Investigation

BY KRISHNA POKHAREL AND PAUL BECKETT

PACHWARA, India—"Where is Sister Valsa?" they demanded. "Where is Sister Valsa?"

In the dark of night on November 15, 2011, the mob surrounded the tile-roof compound. They carried bows and arrows, spades, axes, iron rods.

"I don't have that information," replied a woman who lived in the house, according to a statement she later gave to a local court.

You're lying, she was told.

In one corner of a tiny windowless room off an inner courtyard, Valsa John Malamel, a Christian nun, hid under a blanket punching numbers into her cell phone.

"Some men have surrounded my house, and I am suspecting something foul," she whispered to a journalist friend who lived several hours' drive away.

"Escape at any cost," he said he told her. The call was logged at 10:30 P.M.

She called a friend who lived in the same village. "I have been surrounded on all sides," she told him, according to his court statement. Then the line went dead.

1

The Lust

The landscape of the Rajmahal Hills in the eastern
Indian state of Jharkhand unfolds in a scruffy mix of deep-
red soil, small fields of brown grass, clusters of banana,
ficus, and palm trees, and ponds of murky brown water. It
is the heartland of the Santhal and Paharia, two of India's
indigenous tribes.

There are small signs of modern life here. Tribe members carry cell phones. A satellite dish sits on the occasional
roof. But ancient, pastoral ways persist. The men hunt
rabbit with bows and arrows.

Pachwara is located in the center of the tribal region.
The village of about 3,000 stretches for miles. The houses
are small compounds surrounded by rickety wooden
fences, laundry scattered across the slats. Roofs of red tile
or thatch extend almost to the ground. The walls, once
white or light blue, are spattered with clay. Pigs and piglets,

goats and kids, chickens and chicks, cows and calves, roam and rummage in the mud and leaves. Children, trousers and shoes optional, play on the pathways.

On November 7, 2011, Surajmuni Hembrom, a 22-year-old woman with thick eyebrows and a gold stud in her nose, says she set out on foot with her aunt from Pachwara. They headed for a weekly market to buy groceries. After shopping, they took in a bull fight, a favorite pastime of the tribes. Then they started for home, she says.

At a crossroads, they encountered Adwin Murmu, a 24-year-old college student, and three of his friends, she says. The men started teasing Surajmuni and urged her to join them.

"Why would I, since I don't know you?" she says she responded.

One of the men caught her by the hand and pulled her onto a motorbike between him and Mr. Murmu, she says. Her aunt tried to intervene but was pushed away. Surajmuni Hembrom says the men drove her to an abandoned house and left her alone with Mr. Murmu. He pushed her inside, she says, and locked the door.

Then, she contends, "he raped me all night." (Surajmuni Hembrom gave her consent to be named in this account.)

Surajmuni's father, an oil and rice dealer in Pachwara, says he and his wife searched that night for their daughter. After a hint from a family friend that she had been seen with Adwin Murmu, from the neighboring village of Alubera, the couple walked for two hours before dawn to confront Adwin Murmu's parents.

Adwin's father says he told them his son had not brought Surajmuni to the house. He says his son was "tricked into" spending the night with her by his friends. A lawyer for Adwin Murmu says his client didn't commit rape. Police say the friends are on the run; they couldn't be reached for comment.

Mayur Patel Kanaiyalal, superintendent of police for Pakur district, which includes the villages of Pachwara and Alubera, says he believes the incident took place, but whether it was "with or without consent is still to be investigated."

Later that day, Surajmuni Hembrom was reunited with her parents. They turned to the person from whom villagers had sought guidance for years: Sister Valsa John Malamel.

With a broad jaw and her hair pulled back behind her head, Sister Valsa was 53 years old and a member of the Sisters of Charity of Jesus and Mary, a Belgium-based order of nuns. Surajmuni Hembrom, 31 years her junior, was saving four dollars a week in the hope of opening a tailoring business in the village. Despite their differences, the two were especially close.

Surajmuni spent her free time at the compound where Sister Valsa stayed, cooking for her, washing her clothes, and frequently spending the night. If Sister Valsa found something funny in the newspaper, she read it aloud to Surajmuni. They laughed about a family in Mizoram state, in India's northeast, that had 170 members and ate 50 chickens and 50 kilograms of potatoes for one meal.

After the rape, Sister Valsa's advice was for Surajmuni Hembrom's family first to meet with the tribal chiefs, says Surajmuni's father.

But, he says, the tribal chiefs said that Sister Valsa would decide what to do next. She advised the family to file a complaint at the local police station, seven kilometers away.

On November 9, 2011, the family and three other villagers went to the police. The officer in charge was Chandrika Paswan. He was standing in for the station chief, who was absent that day. Mr. Paswan refused to accept the family's complaint. He says in an interview he wasn't authorized to do so in the absence of his boss. "I told them to settle the matter within their community," he said.

The villagers returned home. Later that day, Adwin Murmu and his parents showed up at the Hembroms' house with five villagers and two sons of the local tribal chiefs, both families confirm.

"We are ready to bring Surajmuni to our home as Adwin's bride," Adwin's father says he told the family.

"You want our daughter to marry a criminal?" Surajmuni's father responded.

On the morning of November 15, Surajmuni Hembrom and her parents returned to the local police station with 13 villagers. The station chief, Banarsi Prasad, also refused to accept their petition, the villagers say.

Instead, they say, he introduced them to a broker, who asked the family to accept 50,000 rupees (about $1,000) to settle the matter. The family refused.

The broker confirms the meeting but says he didn't offer any money. He says he was trying to end the dispute between the families at the request of the police.

Mr. Prasad, the station chief, denies being at the police station that day, saying he was away for police training. He also denies asking a broker to intervene. He claims that, over the phone, he ordered that Surajmuni's complaint be accepted.

However, his subordinate, Mr. Paswan, says both his boss and the broker were present and that Mr. Prasad, the chief, dealt directly with Surajmuni and the broker.

Dejected, the villagers returned to Sister Valsa's house to talk about what to do next. They left around 4:00 P.M. A few hours later, the mob gathered.

2

The Faith

Valsa John Malamel was born in 1958, the seventh child of affluent Christian parents in the southern Indian state of Kerala. She attended a local church regularly as a child.

She studied economics at university in Kochi, a major Keralan port city, and taught at a local school. She was inspired by the work of two nuns from a nearby convent run by the Sisters of Charity of Jesus and Mary, say family members.

Her father, a metals company employee who later became a politician, died of a heart attack in 1982. Sister Valsa took it especially hard.

The next year, after graduating, she signed up for the Roman Catholic order of nuns, which was founded in Belgium in 1803 to serve "the poor and the abandoned," its website says. Out of almost 2,000 nuns, about 400 are

Indian. The order runs 55 convents in India, 24 of them in the state of Jharkhand. They are overseen by a provincial office in Ranchi, the state capital.

Sister Valsa first worked in Jharkhand, which was then part of Bihar state, in the late 1980s. A decade later, she was living and teaching at a convent and school in the Jharkhand town of Amrapara. In her spare time she roamed the fields and streams around the village of Pachwara, according to her sisters in the order and family members.

On her rambles, she became friendly with local tribe members—and increasingly sympathetic to the poverty she witnessed there.

In 1998, Sister Valsa moved out of the Amrapara convent and into Pachwara for good. Here she stayed, having apparently found a place where she could accomplish her mission in life: helping and educating the poor.

She moved into a room in the home of Binej Hembrom. He is the traditional head, or *parganaith*, of 32 tribal villages including Pachwara. (Many of the villagers share Hembrom as a surname.)

The family already had abandoned the Santhal tribe's traditional religion to become Protestant Christians. But Binej Hembrom, 80 years old and almost deaf, continues to fulfill his role as tribal chief during ceremonies and rituals. Those include invoking a deity called Sing Bonga in a grove of native sal trees.

Sister Valsa "was doing good for the village," says Binej Hembrom as he huddled in a blanket in front of the fire in his courtyard.

Sister Valsa did not proselytize, villagers say; there are only a handful of Christians in Pachwara. But she lived as the villagers lived and learned their tribal language, Santhali. She also encouraged them to change their ways.

At the time, adults in the village drank hooch made from the dry husk of the native Mahua tree, says Sonea Deheri, a friend of Sister Valsa. Drunk men fought each other for women.

Mr. Deheri says Sister Valsa persuaded him, his wife, and others to stop drinking alcohol. "She would say to us, 'Follow your culture but live well.'"

Around 2000, Sister Valsa helped the villagers construct their own school, a thatched hut that sits in an open field. She taught there for six years. Today it is attended by about 170 children.

"We used to live like wild animals," remembers Surajmuni Hembrom, who says she was 12 years old when she met Sister Valsa. "But after Sister's arrival, we learned about living a good life."

As Sister Valsa visited villagers to persuade them to send their children to the new school, she caught wind of a government survey being conducted of Pachwara and eight other villages for coal reserves, says Shaji Joseph, editor in chief of *The Public Agenda*, a Hindi-language biweekly published from Ranchi.

In an interview he conducted in 2002, Mr. Joseph says Sister Valsa talked about a company that was planning to mine in the area—and of the destitution she felt had been wrought on tribal life by mining projects in other parts of the state.

Jharkhand gained its statehood in 2000 to give greater representation to tribes who had lived there for thousands of years. The state's name means "forest tract," and more than 30 tribal groups, including the Santhal and Paharia, make up about 28 percent of the state's total population of 33 million.

During colonial days, the tribes in Jharkhand mounted several unsuccessful rebellions against the British, who extended their authority to the region in 1765. The British constructed a vast network of railway lines to ship minerals to Kolkata, the original capital of British India, and onward to England to fuel the nation's booming industrialization.

Jharkhand today is one of the poorest states in India, despite being rich in coal and minerals such as uranium and iron ore. Pachwara and eight other nearby villages have combined coal reserves of 562 million tons, according to the coal ministry in Delhi. The surrounding Rajmahal Hills area has reserves totaling 14.1 billion tons.

It wasn't long before the government of the new state sought to extract that coal. It leased out 1,152 hectares of agricultural and forest land to Panem Coal Mines Ltd. a joint venture between the government-run Punjab State Electricity Board and the privately run Eastern Minerals and Trading Agency of Kolkata.

The company came to the Pachwara area in 2002. It planned to supply coal to thermal power plants in the state of Punjab, about 1,200 kilometers northwest, said Bishwanath Dutta, Panem's director, in an interview.

The villagers mounted a dogged resistance. Their organization was called the Rajmahal Pahar Bachao Andolan, or "Rajmahal Hills Protection Movement." Sister Valsa played a central role as an organizer. Her work rallying the opposition was a turning point in her relationship with the village. It initially strengthened her bond with villagers (and theirs with her) but it also set the course for future friction.

Villagers chased away company officials when they visited the area. They barricaded the roads with bamboo gates. They stopped police and government officials from entering the village. They kept vigil with bows and arrows.

In 2003, as the standoff intensified, the villagers filed a petition before the Jharkhand High Court. They claimed they had special rights under a 1949 law that prevents the transfer and sale of tribal land to those from outside the community. They also claimed the government's action was against their customary right of self-rule, according to court documents.

Two years later, the court ruled against the village's claims. It said the 1949 law doesn't stop the government from using its "right of eminent domain," the power to acquire any private property for public purpose with compensation to the owner.

Sister Valsa and other activists appealed to the Supreme Court of India. Meanwhile, the company started negotiations for a settlement. It already had won over one village near Pachwara, by offering higher compensation than the government. It started mining there in late 2005, says Mr. Dutta, Panem's director.

The other villages saw little option but to negotiate: They figured the Supreme Court would uphold the Jharkhand court ruling and that support would wane as company funds were distributed, villagers say.

Sister Valsa acted as an intermediary. The two sides reached an agreement in November 2006.

The company promised to provide displaced villagers with alternative shelter and regular income in proportion to the land they lost. It promised a share of mining profits plus schools, a hospital, and a job to a member of each family. And as the company moved through the area and tapped out coal seams, there were provisions to return the land, restored to cultivable condition, to the original inhabitants before a new mine could open.

In return, the villagers withdrew their court appeal, and the Supreme Court made a copy of the agreement part of its records. The central government has since proposed a law that would require mining companies to give equity and royalties to those affected by mines.

Binej Hembrom, the *parganaith*, signed the agreement on behalf of nine villages. He also headed a committee to oversee the agreement's implementation. The other members included Sister Valsa and the tribal chiefs of all nine area villages.

The company began distributing a total of 7 million rupees (about $140,000) yearly to displaced families. Sister

Valsa supervised the distribution of the money, according to the company and villagers. Most families in the area earn less than $150 a month, villagers say.

Mining money in the past few years has enriched many villagers. Some new amenities have been built. But the company's arrival, and the protest movement it sparked, were to take a toll on many other aspects of life in Pachwara.

3

The Greed

As Sister Valsa became more involved in the anti-mining protest movement her relationship frayed with her religious order, the Sisters of Charity of Jesus and Mary.

In the early years that she lived in Pachwara, she used to visit the order's nearby convent in Amrapara every weekend. But her visits ceased in 2006. "She found she didn't have the time," says Sister Lilly Pallipurath, who heads the order's council that oversees the Jharkhand convents from Ranchi, the state capital.

The council summoned Sister Valsa to discuss her absence. It suggested placing her elsewhere. She refused.

Sister Valsa's church attendance also lagged, though she told her sisters she celebrated the Eucharist when a local priest visited. The sisters worried that she was neglecting her nun's rituals.

"We always said we approve of her work, but about her religious life we were not very happy," says Sister Lilly, 50 years old.

Sister Valsa would respond, "What is important for me is the life of the people."

But was Sister Valsa losing her faith?

"If you look at rituals and other things, one would say she had no faith," says Sister Lilly. "But rituals and timely prayers are not really faith. That she diminished in her faith, I cannot say that. She always felt close to Jesus."

Sister Valsa also believed her work was closer to the order's original mission of serving the poor than the life her sisters led inside their convents. And she wasn't shy about saying so.

"'I am living the life our founder lived,' she would say," says Sister Lilly. "She felt she was living it much more than the other sisters. I said, 'You can't say that.' That was not appreciated."

In Pachwara, too, resentment was building toward Sister Valsa.

Promodini Hembrom is the 42-year-old niece of Binej Hembrom, the tribal chief, and the daughter of his brother, Cornelious. She says that as Sister Valsa's role as an activist increased, her father and uncle worked at the nun's "beck and call, out of their goodness and ignorance."

"We used to tell our fathers, 'You are the head of the villages; how can an outsider make you run like her dogs here and there?'" Promodini Hembrom says. "But they wouldn't listen. She had made everybody in the village dumb."

Cornelious Hembrom, 73 years old, says he and his brother supported and helped Sister Valsa because they believed she was "working for the good of the village."

After the village reached the 2006 agreement with Panem, Pachwara was undisturbed by the company's activities. But Panem opened two mines in the area, one in Kathaldih, about seven kilometers from Pachwara, where the effects of mining were impossible to escape.

The mine's entrance is a craggy and desolate terrain of black and gray shiny sludge. Dump trucks and coal trucks roar along the access road. A narrower road leads up a few hundred yards past machinery, workers' housing, and piles of trash to the company's offices. Of the almost 600 people employed at Kathaldih, about 400 are local tribal members, a company official says.

The mining takes places in a vast canyon. Its walls are layered like a Himalayan mountainside but they are devoid of green. On the canyon floor, solitary dots of yellow and orange—a mammoth excavating machine, backhoes and trucks—plow through the freshly blasted earth to extract, load and remove the coal.

The road from the mine to the railway station in the nearby city of Pakur is in constant use. Dozens of trucks move slowly in giant convoys. Traffic jams are frequent as the trucks meet convoys returning to the pit.

As the trucks trundle by, local men play out a gruesome ritual of desperate poverty. They line the roadside, waiting for their moment. When it comes, they climb the walls of a passing truck and throw out what coal they can grab from the high pile in the truck bed. The drivers make no effort to stop them. Back on the roadside, the scavengers scrape up the fallen coal with a long fork, pack it into tall sacks, mount the sacks on bicycles, and push them to market to sell as fuel in tea stalls or homes.

In the early hours of the morning, local women line the roads to scrape up bare-handed what the men leave behind, their blackened fingers probing the deep coal dust for a nugget. Everything, even the garbage, is plastered with soot.

Since 2005, more than 150 villagers have died after being hit by coal trucks, according to the villagers and police officials. Bishwanath Dutta, director of Panem, says the transportation of coal is handled by contractors from Pachwara and elsewhere in Jharkhand, and the company doesn't have direct knowledge of these incidents.

The mine has attracted the attention also of local Maoist rebels. They are known as Naxalites, after the village of Naxalbari in the neighboring state of West Bengal, where their insurrection started in 1967. The rebels seek the overthrow of the Indian state and have won support among some tribal villagers in Jharkhand and across central India where government services are decrepit or don't exist. The rebels intimidate villages they view as unsympathetic to their cause. And they target police stations and corporate offices.

In 2009, two senior Panem officials were shot dead while on a morning walk. The murders are under investigation. Police suspect the rebels. On January 10, 2012, a group of about 20 Maoists attacked the Kathaldih mine, firing indiscriminately. They killed a security guard, police say.

By early 2011, villagers in Pachwara and surrounding hamlets had earned unprecedented sums through road construction contracts and other benefits offered by the mining company. But Sister Valsa was growing frustrated. She believed Panem was dragging its feet on key provisions of the 2006 agreement that she had helped negotiate, according to villagers and her friends.

In a May 2011 meeting of the committee that oversees the pact, she demanded that the company build the hospital that, in 2006, it promised to complete by the end of 2007, says James Murmu, a Panem official who was present at the meeting. He says the company took her demand seriously and has acquired land where the hospital will soon be constructed.

Sister Valsa also was coming into increasing conflict with Pycil Hembrom, the 40-year-old son of Binej, the tribal chief, according to Sister Valsa's friend Sonea Deheri and to police documents filed later.

Pycil Hembrom was responsible for distributing company funds to villagers, a process Sister Valsa supervised. But by early 2011, he had begun challenging Sister Valsa's supervisory role, Mr. Deheri says, and sought to usurp her.

He says Pycil Hembrom wanted to have "complete control" of the process of negotiating with the company, distributing company funds for compensation and welfare programs, dispensing contracts and supervising implementation of the 2006 agreement. The contracts and compensation were set to increase dramatically when mining began in Pachwara.

Pycil Hembrom was not available for comment. His son, Prem Hembrom, says his father negotiated with the company only when Sister Valsa was away from the village. He added that his father didn't "want anything for himself from the company."

The differences between Sister Valsa and Pycil Hembrom caused a broader rift between the villagers. And this left Sister Valsa in a difficult position: since she had arrived in Pachwara, she had been staying at the home of Pycil Hembrom's family, where he also lived.

The atmosphere in their shared house soured. Father Tom Kavalakatt, a local priest, says Sister Valsa recounted to him an incident when Pycil Hembrom and his elder brother, Anand, were drinking at the house. Anand Hembrom verbally abused Sister Valsa, Father Tom says she told him.

She confided in her friend Mr. Deheri, too. In a statement later filed with a local court, Mr. Deheri said Sister Valsa told him around that time, "Pycil has started using abusive words against me and is hurting me emotionally."

In late June 2011, Sister Valsa moved out of the house to a pair of small rooms in a nearby home.

Anand Hembrom denies that he or his brother abused Sister Valsa. He says Sister Valsa "went out of the house peacefully." But her relations with the village's most powerful family would never be repaired.

4

The Brutality

In July 2011, Sister Valsa left Jharkhand for Kochi, in Kerala. She went to visit her elder brother, who was suffering from cancer. On August 1, he died.

That evening, Sister Valsa phoned her old friend Sister Sudha Varghese, a nun from a different order who runs a girls' hostel in Patna, the capital of the state of Bihar.

"She was really down emotionally and physically," Sister Sudha says of Sister Valsa. Sister Sudha asked her to visit. Sister Valsa accepted and arrived in Patna in late August 2011. She stayed for the next two months.

Sister Valsa spent her days meeting the girls in the hostel and reading books and newspapers. She was weak from chronic malaria and was recovering from typhoid, Sister Sudha says.

Sister Valsa lamented the state of affairs in Pachwara and expressed growing doubts about the mining company's motives, say Sister Sudha and other friends.

"She said she was getting in the company's way, and the company was trying to split the group that she had successfully built over the years into two," says Sister Sudha. Bishwanath Dutta, director of Panem, denies the allegation.

In the evenings, Sister Valsa talked with her friends in Pachwara by phone. The news was not good.

"*Didi*"—meaning "elder sister" in Hindi—"the villagers are speaking against you, so you have to be cautious," her friend Sonea Deheri says he told Sister Valsa in one call. He told her that he had heard threats made against her life.

"I haven't done anything wrong," he says she responded. "I haven't robbed any money. I am doing service. As long as people want me there, I will be there."

Before she left Patna, Sister Valsa said to Sister Sudha, "Anything can happen to me."

Sister Valsa returned to Pachwara on November 7, 2011. Several villagers say Pycil Hembrom organized a blockade that night that stopped trucks from transporting coal from Panem's mine in nearby Kathaldih. Their aim: to pressure Panem into intervening and asking Sister Valsa to leave the village for good.

Mr. Dutta, director of Panem, says he talked by phone to Pycil Hembrom the next morning. "It happened while we were drunk and we will open the road immediately," Pycil Hembrom said, according to Dutta.

Sajal Kumar Ghosh, a lawyer for Pycil Hembrom, confirms Pycil's involvement in the blockade but says he doesn't know about his client's conversation with Mr. Dutta.

Pycil Hembrom's cousin Promodini Hembrom says Pycil and other family members wanted Sister Valsa to stay away because they didn't want her interfering in villagers' dealings with Panem.

The same night as the blockade, Surajmuni Hembrom, Sister Valsa's closest friend in the village, says she was raped by Adwin Murmu.

"He tortured and raped me throughout the night," she later told police. At 4:00 the next morning, Adwin Murmu pulled her out of the house where the alleged incident took place and said, "Run away quickly," she says.

Sister Valsa recommended that Surajmuni Hembrom and her family file a complaint with the police. Over the next week, they were rebuffed twice at the local police station, according to Surajmuni Hembrom, her parents, and villagers who accompanied them.

On the afternoon of November 15, 2011, Sister Valsa and other friends met at Sister Valsa's place.

It is a small tile-roof compound she shared with a family. Inside the compound's bamboo gate, an outer courtyard leads to a small passageway where pigeons nest in broken cooking pots tied to the ceiling. The passageway leads to an inner courtyard. Off that courtyard are the living quarters.

The friends talked about what Surajmuni Hembrom should do next to ensure that her rape complaint was registered. Then they dispersed at around 4:00 P.M.

Two hours later, Sister Valsa called her journalist friend Shaji Joseph for advice, Mr. Joseph says. He says he suggested that Sister Valsa ask Surajmuni's family to go to the deputy commissioner (the head administrator) of Pakur district, the area that includes Pachwara.

Later that evening, Sunil Kumar Singh, the deputy commissioner, says he got a call from an acquaintance of Sister Valsa's who told him about the police refusal to register the rape complaint.

"I told the caller to bring the girl to my office the next day at twelve thirty," Mr. Singh said in an interview.

At 8:00 P.M., Sister Valsa called her friend Sonea Deheri to ask him to prepare to leave for Mr. Singh's office the next morning with Surajmuni Hembrom and about a dozen villagers, Mr. Deheri says. He says he called around to alert the group, then went to sleep.

Back at the compound, Sister Valsa and Surajmuni Hembrom ate dinner together and had a bedside chat.

"She comforted me, saying 'If we tread on the path of truth, God will be on our side,'" Surajmuni Hembrom says. They turned in for the night in two different rooms at around 10:00, she says. It would be the last time the two friends saw each other.

Not long after, Sonaram Hembrom, whose family lived in the house, returned from his shift as a dump truck driver at the Kathaldih mine.

"All of a sudden there was a powerful push on the door," he said in a statement filed later in a local court. About 40 men, armed with primitive weapons—rods, axes, spades—barged into the outer courtyard, which was lit by a partial moon.

Several men pushed farther into the compound. Among them, according to the court statements of three witnesses, were Pycil Hembrom and Adwin Murmu, the man who had allegedly raped Surajumi Hembrom.

"Where is Sister Valsa?" Adwin Murmu demanded, according to Sonaram Hembrom's statement.

"I don't know," Mr. Hembrom replied. "I just came back from duty."

"If you don't tell, we will kill you," an unidentified voice threatened.

In her small, dark bedroom, Sister Valsa cowered under a blanket. She made frantic calls on her cell phone. The compound was surrounded, she told two friends.

Then, witnesses testified, a voice in the compound shouted, "Found her."

Then there were shouts of "Cut her. Cut her."

The attackers slashed at Sister Valsa in the doorway separating her two rooms. They cut her from above her left ear to her mouth and on her throat. Then they abandoned her bleeding body in the doorway.

As they fled, they blew whistles, burst firecrackers and shouted, "*Inqalaab Jindabad*"—"Long Live the Revolution." Near Sister Valsa's body were scattered a few hand-painted posters, witnesses said.

Soon after, her friend Sonea Deheri rushed in with other villagers. "When we reached, we saw Sister Valsa was dead," he later testified.

A lawyer for Pycil Hembrom, Adwin Murmu, and five other men allegedly involved says his clients played no part in Sister Valsa's death.

Word about the murder spread quickly. About 90 minutes later, Gautam Kumar Samanta, a survey officer with Panem, appeared at the house with Pycil Hembrom and several other villagers.

In an interview, Mr. Samanta says he went with Pycil Hembrom because Mr. Hembrom "is closely associated with the company and is the son of the *parganaith*, who is the last word for any matter in the tribal area."

They stayed at the compound only 10 to 15 seconds, Mr. Samanta says. But before he left, he collected the posters strewn near Sister Valsa's body.

Each poster was 1.5 by 1.5 feet in size, hand-painted with red ink, he says. They read in Hindi: stop looting the people. punjab's panem go back. sister valsa is deceiving the people. communist party of india (maoist).

Mr. Samanta says he took the posters to prevent "terror among the villagers."

He says he also called the police. They refused to come, saying they had orders not to enter the area at night because of the threat of a Naxalite attack. The next morning, Mr. Samanta says, he gave the police the four posters he had taken from the site of Sister Valsa's murder.

5

The Friendship

Arun Oraon, the inspector general of police for the state of Jharkhand, oversaw the probe into Sister Valsa's death. He says police have a theory that three different motives brought together the mob that killed her on the night of November 15, 2011.

First, Adwin Murmu had allegedly raped Sister Valsa's friend Surajmuni Hembrom the previous week. He may have known that Surajmuni and her family, at Sister Valsa's urging, were scheduled to visit the area's most senior bureaucrat on November 16 after police refused to accept Surajmuni's rape complaint, Mr. Oraon says in an interview.

Second, Pycil Hembrom, the son of the tribal chief, and others were fed up with what they viewed as Sister Valsa's interference in their ability to negotiate directly with the local mining company, Panem, Mr. Oraon says.

Six of the seven suspects, including Pycil Hembrom, hold contracts from the company, ranging from housing and road construction to the transportation of coal from the nearby Kathaldih mine, according to the suspects' lawyer and Gautam Kumar Samanta, the senior Panem official.

"Pycil and others thought they will make maximum money in the absence of Sister Valsa's supervision and monitoring," Mr. Oraon says.

Finally, police believe there were perhaps two dozen Naxalites in the mob when Sister Valsa was killed. The rebels may have wanted to create "fear psychosis" among the villagers so they would join the rebel movement, Mr. Oraon says. He notes that in the wake of Sister Valsa's murder, many villagers abandoned their houses and hid in the forests after police began investigating.

"That's the rebels' strategy: to get villagers to support them by creating an environment of distrust and fear of government authorities," he says.

On November 17, two days after Sister Valsa's murder, police finally accepted Surajmuni Hembrom's rape complaint against Adwin Murmu.

On November 18, Jharkhand police suspended Banarsi Prasad, the local police chief, for dereliction of duty and launched an internal inquiry into his conduct. Mr. Oraon says that it was Mr. Prasad's duty to ensure that

Surajmuni Hembrom's rape complaint was registered the first time she tried to make it.

In mid-2012, the internal inquiry by the Jharkhand state police found that both Mr. Prasad and his subordinate, Chandrika Paswan, had failed to do their duty by refusing Surajmuni Hembrom's rape complaint when she first reported it, according to Mr. Oraon. The officers have been denied salary raises or promotions for three years. Mr. Prasad has since moved to another police station and couldn't be reached for comment.

Mr. Paswan, who continues to serve at the same police station near Pachwara, says he has been unfairly punished for Mr. Prasad's inaction. But he says he now realizes, "I should have handled the issue more carefully when it was before me," adding that he now accepts rape and other complaints promptly.

On November 19 and 20, 2011, police arrested Pycil Hembrom, Adwin Murmu, and five others from the villages of Pachwara and nearby Alubera in connection with their alleged involvement in Sister Valsa's murder.

On November 21, police filed a petition with a local court asking that the suspects be remanded in judicial custody. In the petition, the police say the suspects confessed to "having killed Sister Valsa due to money disputes and other disputes in the past."

Sajal Kumar Ghosh, the lawyer representing all of them, says the police have not been able to establish any "intention behind the murder."

Mr. Ghosh says his clients were tortured by police to make false confessions. He also notes that confessions before the police aren't permissible in Indian court cases. He says all his clients are innocent.

Promodini Hembrom, Pycil Hembrom's cousin, says she visited him in jail. She says the men also told her they were "excessively tortured by policemen to make false confessions."

She says the seven accused were friends who "liked to eat, drink and party but they are not the ones who would kill anybody."

Mr. Oraon denies police coerced the suspects into falsely confessing. On November 21, a local Maoist commander, Ramesh Soren, denied in phone calls to reporters that the rebels were involved in the murder, according to Manohar Lal, a local reporter for *The Pioneer* newspaper, who received a call.

Mr. Oraon, the police official, says Mr. Soren is a new member of the Maoists and that the rebels who were at the Pachwara compound were directed from a higher level of the organization.

G. S. Rath, the director general of Jharkhand police, says police also are looking into whether Panem played a role in Sister Valsa's murder.

Bishwanath Dutta denies any company participation. "The allegations by the people that the company had connived to kill Sister Valsa are totally absurd," he said.

As of mid-January 2012, Sister Valsa's rooms in the small compound where she lived in Pachwara were largely untouched, although the site of her murder had been cleaned of blood.

A large metal trunk and a red plastic table occupy the first room, a 10-by-10-foot square. On one wall, a plank suspended from the ceiling by rope holds crumpled copies of a newspaper from November 14, 2011, the day before Sister Valsa was killed. A shelf on another wall holds small pots of coconut hair oil, calamine lotion, and Ponds cold cream.

The second room is near pitch black. A candle illuminates a charpoy—a low wooden bed with stretched cloth strips for a mattress—as well as a small gas stove with two burners, jars of herbs and powdered spices, and a large box of Nestlé creamer.

Sister Valsa was buried in a public Christian cemetery in the town of Dumka, two hours' drive from Pachwara. About 700 villagers, nuns, and priests attended the funeral, including 30 nuns from the Sisters of Charity of Jesus and Mary.

In a prayer at the funeral service, the congregation said, "We believe that she has returned to the Heavenly Father after completing her mission here on Earth."

A simple wooden cross was stuck in the large pile of reddish-brown soil that covered Sister Valsa's grave. Nowhere did the grave bear her name.

Back in Pachwara, Surajmuni Hembrom's father says he is looking for "a suitable man who agrees to marry with Surajmuni after knowing all that has happened to her."

But he says he doubts any man will come forward. "We are ready to keep her with us all our life," he says.

Surajmuni Hembrom says she has been hiding at relatives' houses out of fear. "Had Sister Valsa been here, I would have been fearless," she says. She still wants to train as a seamstress. But as twilight descended on the village, she tended to a small herd of cows with a switch. She wore a plaid shawl against the winter chill.

"Whenever she used to be with me and be free, we had lots of fun," she says of Sister Valsa.

Then Surajmuni Hembrom, and the cows, wandered away.

Epilogue

"When You Are at Home"

On February 16, 2012, police in Jharkhand filed charges, including murder and trespass, against seven men in connection with the death of Sister Valsa. They include Pycil Hembrom, son of the tribal chief of Pachwara village; and Adwin Murmu, who also has been charged with raping Surajmuni Hembrom. The seven men were also charged with being members of the banned Maoist rebel movement that is active in the region.

Three months later, police filed the same charges against nine more tribal men from Pachwara and nearby villages.

They all say they are innocent, according to their lawyers and relatives. Six have been released on bail. Ten others, including Mr. Hembrom and Mr. Murmu, are in jail awaiting trial.

The trials have been delayed for more than a year because the court is overburdened with pending cases, a systemic problem in the Indian justice system.

Police continue to investigate the murder of Sister Valsa, and say they are searching for others who were allegedly in the mob that went to her house the night she was killed.

◆

In Pachwara, relations are strained between the villagers and the local mining company, Panem Coal Mines Ltd., say company officials and associates of Sister Valsa.

Villagers are protesting the company's plan to expand its mining operation to two more nearby villages without first fully implementing its 2006 agreement, which Sister Valsa negotiated on behalf of the nine villages, including Pachwara, according to Sonea Deheri.

In April 2013, the company opened the hospital that it had promised to provide to villagers by the end of 2007. The company has yet to fulfill many of its other commitments, including building the schools and providing electricity, water and other amenities to the villages affected by the mining, Mr. Deheri says.

Senior Panem official Gautam Kumar Samanta says the company is working to fulfill its other promises and is moving into only those villages that want its presence. "We are expanding with the full support of the people in these villages," he says. "Those who are protesting aren't the ones really affected."

◆

A separate trial of Mr. Murmu on charges of abduction and rape in connection with the alleged rape of Surajmuni Hembrom started recently.

On March 7, 2013, Surajmuni testified against Mr. Murmu at the district court in Pakur.

For the last nine months, Surajmuni has been training in tailoring at a Christian mission in a neighboring district, where she stays at a hostel with 20 students. She plans to return to her village after she completes her training, to open a tailoring shop, her life's aspiration, at her parent's street-side house in Pachwara.

"She is now getting back her confidence," says Mr. Deheri, who met her recently when she visited the village on vacation.

◆

At Sister Valsa's grave at the public Christian cemetery in the nearby town of Dumka, the Sisters of Charity of Jesus and Mary have erected a tombstone. It was funded by the order's nuns and Sister Valsa's family in Kerala.

On November 15, 2012, the anniversary of Sister Valsa's death, about 500 people—Pachwara residents, priests, nuns, family members, friends and supporters—gathered at her grave. They organized a Eucharist and a memorial service.

On her tombstone is engraved: WHEN YOU ARE AT HOME, TELL THE NEXT GENERATION THAT I HAVE LAID DOWN MY LIFE FOR THEIR BETTER TOMORROW.

PART II

Falak: The True Story of "India's Baby"

BY PAUL BECKETT AND KRISHNA POKHAREL

DELHI—The story of Baby Falak is a close-up look at the underbelly of Indian society: prostitution, human trafficking, bride selling and domestic violence.

It also is the story of a small group of ordinary people—a young mother, a rebellious teenager, a taxi driver, a tire repairman, a lonely graduate—trying to escape the tribulations of their daily lives, and of the people who exploited them, the institutions that failed them, and the people who helped them.

The events that transpired over 10 months, from mid-2011 to early 2012, moved millions, at least briefly, to unprecedented outrage and introspection, as if India were asking itself, "Are we like this only?"

1

Escape from Bihar

There is nothing special about Muzaffarpur. The city's roads have been pummeled, then buried under the weight and dust of pedestrians, bicycles, rickshaws, motorbikes, and SUVs. Its low brick-and-concrete stores are piled high with the brightly colored flotsam of modern Indian life: flip-flops, candy, tobacco packets, plastic water jugs, tarps. In the center of town, the railway station appears as a bastion of permanence. It has a tower, perhaps 50 feet tall, that is painted light pink.

Hop a train here, and one stop to the southeast, after a 20-minute ride through palms, lychee trees and the light gray soil of the Gangetic Plain, you arrive in Silaut, a small depot with archways and a high passenger bridge that connects the two platforms. It's a commuter stop of sorts for villagers who work in the city. And it's a dot on the spiderweb map of India's national railways. About 100 freight and passenger trains roll through daily.

It was here, in early August 2011, that Munni Khatoon, a pretty, petite young woman, boarded a train with her three tiny children. The trip would propel her from the eastern state of Bihar to Delhi, then to Rajasthan, and then to the front pages of the nation's newspapers and the top of its newscasts.

Before setting out for the 9:00 A.M. train to Muzaffarpur that day, Ms. Khatoon told her parents, "My husband has called me to Delhi to stay with him there." This was a lie.

When she met her mother-in-law on the way to the station, she told her, "I am taking my son to the hospital in Muzaffarpur." This wasn't the whole truth.

Rather, she was on her way out for good, after six years of a violent marriage to a local man called Shah Hussain. Several times a week, she says, he banged her head against the brick wall of their house, giving her headaches that persist today. Mr. Hussain says he hit his wife, but not as severely as she contends.

Ms. Khatoon had found her escape route a month before, when she took her son, Golu, to a government hospital in the city for a rabies shot after a dog bit him on the leg.

At the Muzaffarpur station on the way home, a man who looked about 25 years old asked to borrow her mobile phone. "I have to make a missed call," he told her.

The next day, she got a call from a man who introduced himself as Shankar. "I met you at the station," he said. Then, she says, he added out of the blue, "I love you." He told her he wanted to marry her.

"I am a married woman with kids," Ms. Khatoon says she told him. She also confided that she had had an operation that meant she couldn't have any more children. He said he didn't care, and persisted. She was desperate. So she said, "Tell your family members all about me and then talk to me."

That evening, she says, he called back. "My family members agree to it," he said. He asked her to come with him to Delhi. "How come you live in Bihar?" she asked him. He said he was staying with his sister in Muzaffarpur. "I want to see your sister's house," she said.

She used the pretext of a follow-up rabies shot for Golu to take the train from Silaut that August day to visit the home, a small pink house on a side street.

There, she says, she met a plump, friendly, middle-aged woman called Laxmi Devi who said she was Shankar's sister. Ms. Devi later confirmed her account to police.

Ms. Khatoon, who says she was 19 years old at the time, liked the older woman and felt comfortable in the new family. She and the children stayed at the house for a few days. "When Shankar said that he will take me to Delhi, marry me and also take care of my three kids as his own, I thought, 'My life is already a hell but at least by marrying this guy I will get rid of a beastly man and I can give my children a good future in the city,'" Ms. Khatoon said in an interview.

Ms. Devi's adult daughter offered to look after Khusboo, Ms. Khatoon's four-year-old daughter, until the others were settled in Delhi, says Ms. Khatoon. She accepted. The adult daughter couldn't be reached. Then Ms. Khatoon, the other two kids, Ms. Devi and Shankar set out for the Vaishali Superfast Express, a train that runs through the heart of North India before reaching the capital 19 hours and 1,000 kilometers later.

At the station, Ms. Khatoon says Shankar surprised her. "I have some urgent work to do in Muzaffarpur," he told her. "I will come to Delhi by tomorrow morning's train." The others boarded, and the train departed. It was, according to the chief councilman in Ms. Khatoon's village, the first time a village woman had walked out on her husband. And she walked straight into a trap.

◆

As a young girl, Ms. Khatoon's first impression of Shah Hussain, the boy she would marry, was when he showed the village kids a glass case containing a gold-coated necklace, earrings and two gold bangles. A few days later, he sought her out and told her to wear them. She says she was 11 years old; he was a few years older. Later, at a wedding, he told Ms. Khatoon he had given her the jewelry as "an expression of my liking for you, but you couldn't understand." With those words, she says, he won her heart.

The two started seeing each other more. When her father and brothers began planning her wedding to a different man, Ms. Khatoon walked 50 meters down the street and moved into Mr. Hussain's brick hut. She was barely a teenager.

That same night, her father, Mohammed Zainul, called together the village leaders to formalize their union. The family is Muslim, as is Mr. Hussain; Mr. Zainul also invited Hindus.

"I had dreams of a beautiful life when I married Shah Hussain," Ms. Khatoon said. "I had dreams that he will take good care of me, give me nice clothes to wear, keep me in a good house and our kids will live better lives than our own."

But the young couple had broken a cardinal rule of their community. The marriage had not been arranged, or paid for, by Mr. Zainul. It offended his sense of propriety.

"I married all of my other kids with my own money and only Munni chose her own husband," he said, glaring with deep-set eyes made more piercing by his narrow nose.

It also offended his sense of social status. He is a former head gateman for the railway, in charge of a crossing near Silaut, where the train track cuts across the road that leads to their village, a dusty mix of huts, small houses and grocers' stalls called Maripur. His family has lived there for generations. Mr. Hussain's family was newer. And Mr. Zainul has a larger network of brothers and more property in the family. In short, Mr. Zainul's family was higher class.

Ms. Khatoon's mother gave them plates and a rolling pin as gifts. But when Mr. Hussain asked his new father-in-law for 10,000 rupees ($180) for taking his daughter as his bride, Mr. Zainul says he shot back, "You won't get a penny."

◆

Ms. Khatoon speaks in a quiet but husky voice that is at odds with her tiny stature. Her jaw curves to a pointed chin, and her brow is straight, like her mother's, giving her a slightly severe visage that is framed by waist-length black hair.

Mr. Hussain is a muscular man with razor-thin side-burns and light stubble. His teeth are stained with betel juice.

In an interview, he said he had a "good relationship" with his parents-in-law and with his wife. He acknowledged that he beat her "when she was not taking good care of our kids." But he says he didn't beat her as severely as she claims or any more severely than other men in their village beat their wives.

Several men and women in Maripur agree with him, saying that a husband beating his wife is normal. But one female relative of Mr. Hussain's suggested that his violence was of another order. "Any woman would run away in her situation," she said of Ms. Khatoon.

◆

The refusal of money by his father-in-law gnawed at Mr. Hussain, his wife and in-laws say. Days before the birth of their first child, Ms. Khatoon says, the couple fought physically for the first time. She had saved 7,000 rupees ($130) from the money Mr. Hussain gave her for food and other household expenses. She planned to use it for a hospital delivery and to look after the baby.

However, her husband demanded it, she says. She said no. He slapped her and wrenched the money from her, she says. Her mother-in-law intervened to stop the fight. But Mr. Hussain had the money and, Ms. Khatoon says, quickly lost it gambling. The baby, a son nicknamed Golu, was born at home a few days later.

It was the beginning, Ms. Khatoon says, of a campaign of violence. Several times a week, Mr. Hussain slapped her, beat her and pushed her head into a wall, she says.

One afternoon, when Ms. Khatoon was pregnant with their second child, they had another fight. Ms. Khatoon says she was so distressed she covered herself in kerosene and lit a match. Mr. Hussain blew out the match before the fuel caught fire, grabbed the matchbox, pumped water from the well in the back of their house and doused her, she says.

When a group of village women, drawn by the commotion, gathered outside, they told her to think of her son and her unborn baby. She says she told herself then, "Whatever happens, I will take it. I will show him that I can live."

On March 20, 2010, their third child, Sania, a girl, was born. A few days later, Mr. Hussain attacked Ms. Khatoon with a knife, piercing her upper left thigh, his wife says. Her mother says she dressed the wound. Soon after, Ms. Khatoon went to the hospital in Muzaffarpur for a tubal ligation.

When asked about the details Ms. Khatoon provided, Mr. Hussain said, "Who keeps all these things in mind? Things happen and you forget about them over time." He declined further comment.

Ms. Khatoon's relatives didn't intervene in her relationship because she had gone against her father's wishes, she and family members say. She complained about the beatings to the head of the local council, Chandreshwar Prasad Sharma, who, she says, told her, "All families have these kind of problems and you had a love marriage to this guy." Mr. Sharma denies that Ms. Khatoon approached him.

A woman filing for divorce is unknown in the village. Marriage customs there are governed by men and the community's religious beliefs. Ms. Khatoon's father, for one, has two wives, but no wife in the village has two husbands.

◆

For work, Mr. Hussain traveled to the Muzaffarpur train station daily from Silaut, first to sell tea to passengers and then to work in the pantry car of trains. He spent long hours at the station.

One night in late December 2010, according to local police, Mr. Hussain and a friend went with a young girl, perhaps 13 years old, to a secluded area down the track near a red Stop signal. There, the girl claimed to the cops the next morning, they raped her.

Mr. Hussain says he went with two friends and the girl to the spot that night. He says his two friends had sex with her but that he did not. He says he was wrongly included in the girl's rape complaint.

Facing criminal charges, he did what generations of young men from the village had done before him: he bolted for a big city. The rape charges are pending. Muzaffarpur police say they have been unable to locate Mr. Hussain and have characterized him in court documents as "absconding."

Maripur's trade specialty is training boys to fix tires in the cramped shops that line the roadsides of Delhi, Mumbai and Kolkata. Mr. Hussain fled to the capital, where he found work at a tire repair shop in the suburb of Gurgaon that was owned by a friend from the village.

For the first half of 2011, Ms. Khatoon stayed in Maripur and got by the best she could. But she had no money, and she says older men in the village started leering at her.

When she lied to her father in August that she was going to Delhi to be with Mr. Hussain, he didn't try to stop her: "I didn't object because it was a wife going to meet her husband."

◆

On the train, Ms. Khatoon, Laxmi Devi and the two children rode in the more expensive sleeper-class compartment, a promising sign. But along the way, Ms. Devi delivered a blow: she told Ms. Khatoon that Shankar, the man she had tied her future to, was already living with another woman, Ms. Khatoon says.

"Why would he keep you?" Ms. Devi asked Ms. Khatoon.

Ms. Khatoon was stunned. "Why didn't you tell me that Shankar was already married when I was at your home?" she says she asked.

"What would you have done?" Ms. Devi replied. "Could you have gone back to your village?"

Confused, Ms. Khatoon asked what she should do. "Come and stay with me with your kids and do prostitution," she says Ms. Devi told her. "That way, you can look after your kids."

Ms. Devi later said in a confession to police that she and Shankar, whose last name is not known, ran a con. He identified vulnerable women in Bihar, introduced them to Ms. Devi as his sister in Muzaffarpur, then lured them to Delhi with the promise of marriage to supply Ms. Devi's prostitution business.

A lawyer for Ms. Devi says his client has been "falsely implicated," but declined to elaborate. Shankar could not be reached; police say they have been unable to trace him.

Ms. Khatoon says she felt she had little choice, at that point, but to go along. She couldn't face seeking out Mr. Hussain, even though he was in Delhi. She had left her village with 40 rupees (about $0.70), so couldn't get by alone. And her brothers in Delhi wanted nothing to do with her. She also liked the older woman and thought she was genuine in wanting to help her find her feet.

When the train arrived at New Delhi Railway Station, the small group piled into a motorized rickshaw (an inexpensive, three-wheeled taxi). As they rode along the city's wide thoroughfares lined with hulking buildings and teeming with traffic, Ms. Khatoon remembers thinking, "So many people are working and living their lives in this big city. Why can't I?"

They moved into a house in the neighborhood of Uttam Nagar in West Delhi, where Ms. Devi ran a prostitution racket, according to her confession. She also ran a local beauty parlor and a tailoring shop, according to two people who know her.

Ms. Khatoon refused to sell herself, to her host's frustration. Instead, she pleaded to Ms. Devi to find her a new husband. She never saw Shankar again.

Within two weeks, Ms. Devi found a prospective groom, a young man from Rajasthan called Harpal Singh, several people involved say. Ms. Devi told Ms. Khatoon that Mr. Singh already had grown kids, so Ms. Khatoon's inability to conceive wouldn't be an issue. If she went through with the marriage, she could tell her new husband afterward about her past. Ms. Devi said the children would be looked after and then would join their mother in Rajasthan within 15 days.

"I had made Munni agree to the marriage by telling her that I will send her kids back to her later on," Ms. Devi said in her confession.

Ms. Khatoon would say later, after everything happened, that the woman she hated most was Laxmi Devi, but at the time, she felt that Ms. Devi was also the only person looking out for her.

"She used to call me 'beti' [daughter], and I used to call her 'auntie,'" Ms. Khatoon said of their relationship. "She used to give me everything I asked for: food, new clothes. She speaks and behaves in such a way that you can't make out she will do anything to harm you."

In late August, Mr. Singh, the prospective groom, was shown a photo of Ms. Khatoon and told she was a Hindu virgin named Anita.

"There was nothing to like or dislike about her," Mr. Singh said in an interview. His family agreed to take her, unaware that she was already married. They agreed to pay for her, too.

2

A New Life Unravels

Harpal Singh appeared to be a young man of some prospects, a good catch. In 2007, he had graduated with a degree in economics and political science from a college in Jhunjhunu, in Rajasthan, near where he lives with his parents and brother. He was trained to be an electrician but farms wheat and mustard seed on his family land. He owns a tractor and earns up to 20,000 rupees ($360) a month. The family members are Jaats, conservative Hindus.

Mr. Singh can cite the problem that prompted him to jump at the chance, no questions asked, of marrying Munni Khatoon: there weren't enough local women for the local men to marry.

This is the effect of decades of parents favoring male children over female. It is a problem across much of India.

Girl fetuses have been so frequently aborted that sex deter-mination during pregnancy is illegal. But feticide is still rampant in many communities. Locals in the area where Mr. Singh lives say they can just go to Jhunjhunu and dis-pose of unborn girls.

Overall, there are 926 women in Rajasthan for every 1,000 men, according to the 2011 census. That's a slight narrowing of the gap from a decade ago, but the gap for children under 6 years old has widened, to 883 girls for every 1,000 boys, from 909 girls in 2001.

Boys are prized for their earning potential and because, by tradition, they inhabit and inherit the family home. A girl is expected to move in with her in-laws once she is married. The gap in numbers has created a bride shortage in Rajasthan—and a market for young women brought in from other states.

"I know there aren't many girls available for marriage in Rajasthan," Mr. Singh said in an interview. Mr. Singh says the man who played a role in arranging the marriage with Ms. Khatoon was his cousin Amar, who lives nearby.

On the basis of seeing Ms. Khatoon's photo, Mr. Singh agreed to pay, initially, a fee of 200,000 rupees (about $3,600), which was later bumped up by another 75,000 rupees (about $1,360.)

He says he gave the money to Amar after being told that "Anita's" uncle, who was said to live in a Rajasthani village, needed bail money to get out of jail.

Amar Singh agrees that Harpal paid for Anita, but he says he didn't receive any of the payment. "I didn't take money from him for his marriage nor did I know the girl before his marriage," Amar said.

The wedding was set for September 1, 2011, barely three weeks after Ms. Khatoon left her relatives on the other side of the country.

The day before the marriage, Mr. Singh organized a daawat, a huge wedding feast, for 2,000 relatives, friends and others in his community. It cost him 80,000 rupees ($1,450). "Naturally, I was happy and excited about the marriage," he said in an interview. After all, "you don't marry every day."

The following morning, in two Tavera jeeps, relatives and friends set out for the drive from Jhunjhunu to Rohtak, a town in the neighboring state of Haryana, where the wedding was to be held.

Mr. Singh is tall and stick-thin. He towered over his new wife. In their wedding photos, her face is compact; his is a collection of prominent features: jug ears, strong eyebrows and a thin, dapper mustache. He wore a shiny royal blue suit, a matching tie and a red-and-gold patterned turban. Her head was covered with a traditional scarf.

The venue for the wedding was owned by Saroj Chaudhary, a middle-aged woman who walked with a slight limp, Mr. Singh's family members recall.

Laxmi Devi, the woman who sent Ms. Khatoon from Delhi as the bride, said in a later police confession that Ms. Chaudhary was party to the ruse. Ms. Chaudhary could not be reached. Police say she is on the run; they have issued a warrant for her arrest.

◆

The red soil of the Rajasthan countryside that the newlyweds rode through on the way to Harpal Singh's house is billiard-table flat and pocked with short trees. Then, near Jhunjhunu, the landscape becomes more undulating and sandier, a sign of the nearness of the Thar Desert. It is white-hot.

At the top of a small rise is the Singh house. It is an L-shaped building with four bedrooms, a porch, a forecourt and a large yard that holds farm equipment. It is painted pale indigo, the ancient color of Rajasthan. Though basic, it has an occasional design flourish and a satellite television. Some members of the family, though Hindu, follow a Sikh spiritual leader called Sant Rajinder Singh Ji Maharaj.

The couple moved into a bedroom with three woodframe beds and a view over the fields.

At last, Mr. Singh had a wife.

They ate at hotels in Jhunjhunu. He treated her well, they both say. She was cordial with the family and cooked good vegetables and bread.

But she was also frequently aloof and depressed. She would spend time on the roof, looking at the panoramic vista.

When her husband asked her, "Anita, what's the matter?" she answered, "No, it's nothing, I'm fine.'"

She had expected Ms. Chaudhary, who hosted the wedding, to visit within three weeks, in accordance with Hindu custom. But Ms. Chaudhary never showed, she says. And as the days passed, the magnitude of what Munni Khatoon had done crept up on her.

To make the wedding happen and maintain the fiction that she was a virgin, she had handed over custody of her three small kids to people she barely knew.

She says she did it because she didn't know what lay ahead for her, or them. And she says she trusted Ms. Devi, who told her they would be reunited before long. But their absence stung. "I used to remain unwell and used to cry remembering my kids," she said of her first weeks of marriage. She didn't know then that they would never all be together again.

◆

Khusboo, her 4-year-old daughter, hadn't made it to Delhi. Ms. Khatoon says she left her with Laxmi Devi's adult daughter to be looked after in Muzaffarpur. Ms. Devi's daughter couldn't be reached.

Before long, however, Khusboo was living with strangers in a nearby slum, a 20-by-6-foot space that boasts a water pipe but otherwise is strewn with trash, flies and filth. The brick wall that sections off the bedroom has a large, almost circular hole, as if a cannonball hit it.

The 70-year-old woman who lives there says her son, Ghanti Mistry, a van driver in the neighborhood, found the girl crying by a nearby Hindu temple. When no one claimed her, he brought her home as his own, his mother says. His wife had left him two years before, she says, and he wanted a child.

"I kept her and fed her well," the mother said in an interview. But the family knew what they should have done: "She was a missing child, so we should have reported her to the police," said the mother. Her son, Mr. Mistry, 30 years old, couldn't be reached for comment.

◆

The other two children—Golu, a 5-year-old boy, and Sania, an 18-month-old girl—stayed at Laxmi Devi's house in Uttam Nagar in Delhi, according to several accounts.

The neighborhood is like dozens across the city, thriving and clogged. Buildings on the main thoroughfare are three stories high; some have mirrored blue windows. There is a Yamaha scooter showroom, a hookah café, a Baskin-Robbins stand and a billboard offering call center training and "personality development."

About half a kilometer off this main road is the house where the children were put up. It is yellow with brown metal doors and window frames. An internal staircase, visible from the street, leads to a flat roof.

In mid-August 2011, word spread that there was a boy in the neighborhood whose mother was looking for someone to care for him.

Mohammed Sakil, an itinerant garment seller who lives nearby, heard it from his friend Manoj Kumar Nandan, who did odd jobs in the house where the boy was staying, according to several accounts. Mr. Sakil couldn't be reached.

"Do you want a son?" Mr. Sakil's wife says he asked her one day. They have three daughters, ages 18, 12 and 9.

She said yes.

"I have got a boy," he told her.

"It's good if we can get a recently born child," she suggested.

He said the boy was five. His wife said go ahead anyway. In a meeting between Mr. Sakil and Ms. Khatoon to arrange the handover, he asked for something signed, Ms. Khatoon says. She says she refused. He acquiesced—and walked off with Golu. His wife noted in her diary the day he arrived.

"Everybody wants a son," the wife, Aashma Begum, 35, said in an interview. "These daughters go to the houses of their husbands after marriage. If I have a son, he will bring a daughter-in-law and they will look after us when we are old."

Mr. Sakil told Ms. Begum only that he'd gotten the boy from a friend, she says.

The family lives in a warren of shared rooms. They keep chickens—the girls keep one colored bright green, just for fun—a goat and two white pet rats (because they supposedly keep the other rats away.)

The boy was welcomed; the girls played with him. "We also want to have a brother," said Yashmin, the 18-year-old daughter.

Golu was well behaved but restless, the family says. He watched cartoons as soon as he awoke—*Doraemon* and *Oggy and the Cockroaches*. He called the adults "mommy" and "papa" and occasionally demanded of them, "Give me one rupee." He'd take it to buy a toffee at the store. Ms. Begum says she told people in the neighborhood he was her son. The boy said nothing of his mother, sisters, or Bihar, she says. When they asked him what he wanted to be when he grew up, he said, "Policeman."

◆

Sania, Ms. Khatoon's baby girl, stayed the longest in the Uttam Nagar house. A neighbor remembers seeing, from her balcony, a small baby playing on the roof next door.

Sania was cared for by Ms. Devi's cook, Pratima Devi Chatterjee. Ms. Chatterjee, a 55-year-old, fair-skinned Bengali with burn marks on her left hand, has three kids of her own. She and Mr. Nandan, the odd-jobs man, are an item, Ms. Chatterjee says.

Ms. Chatterjee says she called the baby Babu, an affectionate term for a kid.

"You feed her food and milk in time and she would play on her own and sleep," Ms. Chatterjee said in an interview. "She was very close to me."

One day, in the autumn of 2011, she says Laxmi Devi, her boss, told her, "I can't be looking after this child, and her mother hasn't returned, so take her with you."

Mr. Nandan once again found a solution. In addition to doing odd jobs at the house, he drove a taxi. The man who owned the cab was looking for a child.

Later, in the newspapers and in police statements, that man would be called Rajkumar. But, at the time, most people knew him as Mohammed Dilshad, a man in his early thirties who had moved to Delhi a decade before and started driving an auto rickshaw. He often ferried prostitutes around town.

He made enough to purchase a car to use as a taxi. He and his wife paid 8,000 rupees ($145) in monthly rent for a three-bedroom, one-story house in Dwarka, an area on the western reaches of Delhi. He bought a second cab. They were up-and-comers of sorts.

Their 2-year-old son had suffered brain damage, the boy's mother said in an interview, and was cared for mostly by his grandparents near Mumbai. The couple wanted another kid, according to the boy's mother and to a statement Mr. Dilshad later gave police. He could not be reached.

Adopting Sania was the answer. One autumn evening at around 8:00 P.M., Ms. Chatterjee and Mr. Nandan took the girl to Dwarka.

"Keep her well," Ms. Chatterjee told Mr. Dilshad. The couple decided to rename her Falak, Urdu for "sky."

◆

In Jhunjhunu, Harpal Singh was starting to wonder about his new, sad wife. He noticed that when they went to bed, she made sure the lights were off. And she wasn't getting pregnant. Ms. Khatoon told him she had had an appendectomy, so conceiving was a challenge.

After several weeks, Mr. Singh took her to a hospital for a check-up. A doctor explained to him that his wife had had a tubal ligation and could not conceive. Mr. Singh confronted Ms. Khatoon. She confessed. She told him about Bihar, her previous marriage, her three kids.

He was devastated, but too ashamed to tell his relatives. He moved into a separate bedroom. Ms. Khatoon, her cover blown, called Ms. Chaudhary, the woman who had been instrumental in marrying her off.

According to Ms. Khatoon, Ms. Chaudhary advised her to steal all the money and jewelry she could find in the house and escape. Ms. Khatoon refused and told Mr. Singh about it, both say.

Ms. Khatoon told her husband: "I just want to go back to my kids."

3

The Runaway

Gudiya means "doll" in Hindi.

It was the nickname of a tiny 14-year-old girl with a light complexion, long black hair, a round face and eyebrows set ever so slightly toward the sides of her face. She was given the name by the people who sent her to have paid sex with men in neighborhoods on the fringes of South Delhi over five months, starting in June 2011.

◆

Govindpuri is a messy, broiling neighborhood that has little to distinguish it aside from a temple with a gigantic statue of the monkey god, Hanuman. It doesn't display the signs of India's economic growth that neighborhoods just one rung up do. It feels like a place you drive through and don't bother to look around.

As a small child, Gudiya lived with her mother, Pushpa, and an uncle. Her father, Jitender Gupta, says he was imprisoned after being convicted of murdering a relative in 1998.

After Mr. Gupta, 40 years old, was released in 2004, the family moved together to Govindpuri, to a quiet side street not far from the clogged traffic and honking horns around the Hanuman statue.

In 2005, Gudiya's mother died from tuberculosis. Mr. Gupta had to raise their daughter alone.

He is a hawklike little man with forearms so wiry that his veins look like a topographical map. He worked long hours selling cucumbers, eggplants, beans and other vegetables from the roadside near the Hanuman temple.

He struggled with Gudiya. He beat her with his belt and fists, his daughter told authorities. His response, in an interview: I didn't. But if I did, it was for her own good.

Their relationship became so sour that Gudiya was put in an orphanage. She said in a police statement that her father put her there. Mr. Gupta says Gudiya's aunt deceived him into it. Either way, the orphanage was convinced she was parentless. Gudiya stayed for three years.

The orphanage was, in its way, a refuge. Gudiya later told counselors that she was hit hard once on the leg with a stick as punishment after she accidentally opened a bathroom door that hit another girl's head. But, overall, she said, she saw no signs of serial abuse of the children there.

"The girl said that the hostel is a safe place," according to a later counseling report. (That report and others were provided, in redacted form, by Delhi's child protection agency.)

When she was roughly 13, Gudiya had had enough. She walked out. She bounced around various relatives before returning to her father.

They lived in a neighborhood close to Govindpuri called Sangam Vihar, where the streets are lined with banana sellers, shoe repairmen, pastry sellers and women collecting water in large jugs. It feels like a small rural town, one of hundreds stitched together to make up Delhi.

At a crossroads, up a short flight of stairs, Gudiya and her father—plus Mr. Gupta's new girlfriend, a woman named Geeta—lived in one room. It is about 10 feet square, with painted blue walls, a glassless window and a wooden door. It cost 1,000 rupees ($18) a month to rent.

There was close-quarters friction. Mr. Gupta asked his daughter to call Geeta "Mommy," Gudiya said in a court statement. When she refused, she said her father beat her. Geeta split. And on May 26, 2011, saying she feared violence when her father came home drunk, Gudiya, aged 14, took off, too.

Her first stop, according to a statement she later gave before a court, was the All India Institute of Medical Sciences, a top government research hospital, where Geeta worked. (Geeta could not be reached; a judge in the first week of June 2012 asked police to produce her in court. Police said they failed to trace her despite several attempts.)

The older woman took Gudiya to see a woman called Pooja Pandey back in Govindpuri. They were already acquainted: Ms. Pandey knew Gudiya and her father because her husband also ran a vegetable stall in Govindpuri. Gudiya stayed with them.

The couple didn't tell Gudiya's father where she was. A few days after his daughter fled, Jitender Gupta went to the police and filed a missing person report.

◆

Pooja Pandey viewed the young girl as a possible wife for a nephew of hers in the town of Etah, in Uttar Pradesh, the giant, ramshackle state that borders Delhi to the east. She tried to talk Gudiya into the marriage, but the girl balked.

Ms. Pandey presented her with a choice, according to a statement the older woman later gave to police: "You either marry with our nephew or do prostitution."

Gudiya was silent, according to her own later statement to a judge.

That night, Ms. Pandey and her husband, Sandeep, took Gudiya to Mr. Pandey's village, according to an account provided by Gudiya as well as to police statements by the Pandeys. The couple could not be reached for comment.

There, Gudiya saw a young woman about her age who had married an older relative of the Pandeys, according to her statement. The young woman's husband and mother-in-law used to beat her, Gudiya says. She told Ms. Pandey, according to the statement, "I'll do whatever you say, but I won't marry."

That night, Gudiya was given bitter white alcohol to drink. Then Mr. Pandey took her to the roof of the house, made her undress and told her to lie down. Ms. Pandey held Gudiya's hands. Mr. Pandey undressed himself and raped her, according to both women and Mr. Pandey's police statement.

The next morning, the husband and wife returned to Delhi, leaving Gudiya in the village. A month later, Gudiya joined them in Delhi. Mr. Pandey raped her again, repeatedly—and with his wife's knowledge—over three days, according to all three. The couple brought other men to her as well, charging them each 500 rupees ($9), according to the Pandeys' statements and to Gudiya. Gudiya later told a counselor that there were other young girls working at the house, according to the counselor's report.

Engaging in prostitution is not illegal in India, but related activities, such as soliciting and running a brothel, are. Having sex with a minor is considered rape.

Around August 2011, Gudiya was subcontracted out for one week to another couple who ran a prostitution racket, Ms. Pandey's statement said. The deal was that Gudiya was to have sex with seven men a day for seven days, Gudiya later told a counselor.

She also told the counselor that when the woman of the house realized how young she was, the number of days was reduced to four. Gudiya said she had sex with all types of men, young and old, in their houses and in hotels.

◆

Mohammed Dilshad was one of the drivers who took her from appointment to appointment, he later told police.

He is in his early 30s, clean shaven, and about five foot five. He wears his hair long and slick, parted in the middle and brushed back. He was an auto rickshaw driver successful enough to upgrade to two taxis—a Hyundai Accent and a Maruti Zen—and to hire a part-time employee.

That employee was Manoj Kumar Nandan, the man who did odd jobs at Laxmi Devi's house in Uttam Nagar and who had brought Falak to Mr. Dilshad and his wife to raise as their own

Mr. Dilshad and Gudiya hit it off, according to statements made by both.

◆

After her contract was over, Gudiya returned to stay with Pooja Pandey. She told a counselor she earned 20,000 rupees ($360) in four days but saw none of it.

One night, Ms. Pandey, who was pregnant, got labor pains. She told Gudiya to accompany her to hospital. There, while Ms. Pandey was being examined, Gudiya slipped away, according to statements that both made to police.

She returned to the house where she had just been and started working again as a prostitute, her statement said. She saw Mr. Dilshad again. The girl "had started liking me and I had also trapped her in my love," he later said in a statement to police. They began an affair, they both confirmed in statements.

He installed Gudiya in a rented room in his neighborhood. She took clients to make some money. On November 15, 2011, Mr. Dilshad's wife, after a quarrel with him, left for her parents' place in Mumbai. Around that time, Mr. Dilshad and Gudiya performed a marriage ceremony in a temple, even though he remains married to his wife. He called himself Rajkumar.

"After marriage, I didn't do prostitution nor did Rajkumar tell me to do prostitution," Gudiya later said in her court statement.

Around the New Year, he brought her Falak, she told a counselor. Then Mr. Dilshad moved Falak and Gudiya to a guesthouse in a neon-spattered hotel district by the Indira Gandhi International Airport. Soon after, Mr. Dilshad left for Mumbai to see his son, leaving Falak and Gudiya alone.

At first, Gudiya enjoyed the role. She felt Falak was "so sweet little baby," a counseling report said. The kid slept well at night and didn't create problems during the day. In the mornings, Gudiya bathed her then fed her breakfast— bread, butter, biscuits, snacks, milk and tea. She fed her biscuits during the day and cooked rice and lentils at night. She kept her in Huggies diapers. If they needed supplies, Gudiya said she called for delivery or popped out to a local store. Falak played in the room by herself, according to a counseling report.

But each day that passed brought them closer to the events that would pitch them into leading roles in a nationally televised drama.

◆

There is an old woman who still lives on the same side street in Govindpuri where Gudiya stayed when she was younger. "She was a nice girl," the woman recalled. "She was fine."

When asked how she felt about Gudiya today, she replied, "What can I say? You know what happens to a motherless child."

4

The Battering

On the night of January 17, 2012, the baby wouldn't stop crying.

She had started around 10 o'clock and Gudiya couldn't calm her down.

The two girls, roughly 16 years of age between them, were living alone in room 210 of the Shalimar PG guesthouse in Mahipalpur, near the Delhi airport. It was going fine. But in a shambolic neighborhood of transients—contract workers at the new airport terminal, rickshaw drivers, travelers from across India—they were anonymous and invisible.

Residents in the apartment building next door, whose balcony is just a few feet away, say they don't remember ever seeing a young girl with a baby there. Nor do the local shopkeepers, from whom Gudiya said she bought supplies. Even some of the guesthouse's maids say they didn't know there was a child in the room. And no one remembers hearing crying that night.

But 22-month-old Falak, unusually for her, was throwing tantrums.

Gudiya kept trying to quiet her, but it wasn't working, according to an account of the night's events she later gave a counselor.

Then Gudiya snapped.

She slapped Falak three or four times and, crucially for what was to come, she says she bit her. Hard. On both cheeks and on her right leg—so hard she left tooth marks that were identifiably human.

Gudiya's anger subsided. She fed Falak some biscuits, and the baby slept. But half an hour later, she soiled her diaper and awoke.

Gudiya carried Falak to the tiny bathroom adjoining the bedroom to clean her, according to a counseling report. She says she placed Falak standing on the floor next to a bucket. Then she reached for the switch on the hot-water tank. *Thud!* Falak moved suddenly, slipped and fell face-first on the marble floor, according to Gudiya.

Gudiya would claim to others that Falak fell off the bed while both were sleeping, according to those who spoke with her. The result was the same: A deep gash opened in the baby's head. It bled profusely.

Stricken, Gudiya says she went in search of first-aid supplies, leaving the baby alone on the bed. She returned and bandaged Falak's head. The baby fell back to sleep.

But the wound, according to a counseling report, "became bigger and opened up more."

Gudiya says she thought about taking the baby to hospital. But it was the dead of night, and she was a stranger in the neighborhood. Instead, she dialed Mohammed Dilshad, the man she knew as Rajkumar, in Mumbai. On the phone, she asked him what to do.

"It's late in the night; where will you go alone?" he asked her, according to a statement he made later to police. "Take her to the hospital as soon as it's morning."

◆

Even low-rent neighborhoods have lower-rent neighborhoods that service them. For Mahipalpur, that neighborhood is Arjun Camp. The slum is hidden behind valleys of trash and fluffy trees. The roar of jet engines from the planes that land every few minutes on the nearby runway provides another kind of curtain.

Inside, along the narrow lanes, in a tin-roofed, mud-brick room, lives Usha Devi. She is small and sharp-featured and, when she speaks, she pours out a torrent of words.

The encampment has been home to her family—her husband, their two daughters and one son—since 2007. Her husband works as a janitor at a paramilitary installation. Around the beginning of 2012, Ms. Devi, 30 years old, found a job as a cleaner at the Shalimar PG guesthouse. On the morning of January 18, she showed up for work at 9:00 A.M.

As she scrubbed the passageways on the second floor, she needed fresh water. She rang the bell of room 210 to get to a tap. A teenage girl opened the door.

"She was with a baby that was lying on the bed," Ms. Devi said in an interview. "The baby was injured and in serious condition. She had injury marks on the cheek, a deep open gash on the forehead. Her eyes were closed and she was continuously throwing her legs on the bed."

The baby, naked, was also shivering in the winter cold, Ms. Devi says. The minimum temperature in Delhi that day was 5.6 degrees Celsius (42 degrees Fahrenheit).

"What will I do?" the girl muttered as she paced the room, according to Ms. Devi. "The baby got injured. Who will help me?"

"Why don't you take the baby to the hospital?" Ms. Devi says she asked her.

"I don't know any doctor or hospital here," the girl replied. "Please come with me."

"I helped the girl because I felt pain for the baby as any mother would," Ms. Devi later told police. "I also have my own daughter about the same age as that baby. I thought of that baby as my own child when I saw her injured in the room."

In a flurry, Ms. Devi sought the manager's permission to leave, it was granted, and a rickshaw was hailed. Falak was dressed in a cap and socks and wrapped in a woolen scarf that covered all but a sliver of her tiny bruised face. Gudiya, in a black coat, took the baby in her arms, and the three of them climbed into the rickshaw.

The receptionist at a nearby clinic recommended they head for the All India Institute of Medical Sciences (AIIMS), the government research hospital in the center of Delhi.

After a roughly 16-kilometer (10-mile) trip, the small party pulled up to the main gate. They reached the emergency ward but were told to take the baby to another AIIMS facility nearby, called the Jai Prakash Narayan Apex Trauma Center, Ms. Devi says.

Falak was unconscious.

In the early afternoon, at the trauma center, they were met by Dr. Manmeet Kaur.

"My first reaction was 'How can somebody be so cruel to a baby?'" Dr. Kaur said in an interview.

Gudiya declared that she was the baby's mother, but she looked so young that the doctor was skeptical.

As a test, Dr. Kaur asked, "How old is the baby?"

"The baby is four or five months old," replied Gudiya, several witnesses confirm. By her size and weight, Falak was clearly older.

"You don't know the age of your baby?" Dr. Kaur pressed, her suspicions rising. She asked what had happened.

Gudiya blurted out, "The baby didn't cry after falling from bed last night. You talk to my husband. He is in Mumbai."

Gudiya dialed Rajkumar and handed the phone to the doctor. He told her the baby was about 18 months old.

Falak was in critical condition. The hospital staff admitted the baby to the emergency ward. Then they called the police.

EXCERPTS FROM EMERGENCY DEPARTMENT MLC PROGRESS NOTE, 1/18/2012

VISIBLE INJURIES ON PATIENT: VISIBLE WOUND: BRUISE (MULTIPLE ON BODY—BOTH LEGS, ARMS, FACE AND ABDOMEN), SWELLING (DEFORMITY AND CREPITUS BOTH FOREARMS), LACERATION (3x1.5 CM ON FOREHEAD RIGHT SIDE), LACERATION (3x0.5 CM ON CCCIPITAL [SIC] AREA ON SCALP) OTHERS (CIRCULAR BITE MARKS ON BOTH CHEEKS AND RT LEG) SWELLING (RT EYE)

NATURE OF INJURY: PENDING INVESTIGATION

Deepak Agrawal, a 41-year-old neurosurgeon, had seen battered babies before, but in Canada, not India.

The son of an Indian army neurosurgeon, he spent a year training in pediatric neurosurgery at a hospital in Vancouver. He felt like a fish out of water there, detached from his own country and countrymen. But he learned a lot about how children come to be abused—something he had not considered before going overseas.

"I saw lots of children with child abuse; we just expected almost one a month," he said in an interview in his cramped office at the trauma center. "Over here, we had not seen any battered baby syndrome or whatever you call it. We never came across any."

He learned that even rich families batter their kids, so a lack of wealth wasn't at the root of it. Stress was. Which makes him worry for the future of his country as it modernizes. "Maybe as India goes up the ladder and becomes more stressful, we're also going to have the same kind of thing happening," he said.

That afternoon, Dr. Agrawal assessed Falak. He was surprised to find her well fed, given her wounds and what he had heard about the suspicious circumstances of her admission. She was better fed, in fact, than many of the babies who show up at AIIMS, given that it is a government hospital and almost anyone in India who can afford to goes private. "This kid was very healthy," he said.

But she was obviously badly injured. And there was pressure on her brain from a blood clot. Dr. Agrawal decided immediately to perform an operation that would relieve the tension inside her skull.

> **EXCERPTS FROM OPERATION NOTE, 1/18/2012 14:56**
>
> TEMPORAL BONE NIBBLED UP TO THE BASE USING BONE NIBBLER. DURA WAS TENSE, 100 ML MANNITOL INFUSED AND HYPER-VENTILATION GIVEN . . . A "U" SHAPED DURAL FLAP RAISED WITH BASE TOWARDS SUPERIOR SAGGITAL [SIC] SINUS. BRAIN BULGE PRESENT. ACUTE SDH FOUND AND EVACUATED.

The operation took more than four hours in all and ended successfully at 7:00 P.M.

Sometime afterward, a police subinspector and a female constable trudged up a long flight of stairs to an apartment in East Delhi, across the Yamuna River from the main city. Gudiya was with them. They rang the bell.

It was the home of Raaj Mangal Prasad, chairman of Delhi's Child Welfare Committee, an agency charged with looking out for children who need protection.

Mr. Prasad invited them in. "The teenager looked very confused, nervous," he said in an interview. "The subinspector and the other officer looked very exhausted and tense."

The group settled themselves on brown armchairs and sofas in the Prasads' lace-curtained living room. Gudiya sat next to the female police constable.

Mr. Prasad offered samosas and tea. "Only if she has," Gudiya said, pointing to the constable next to her. Mr. Prasad's wife brought the snacks from the kitchen. Then Gudiya began to talk.

5

The Circus

Falak, bruised and unconscious in the intensive care unit, was struggling. Within a week, she had two heart attacks. The doctors treated her, as they were obliged to do, but they figured she was done.

"You do it just for the sake of it, because that's the protocol when you have an arrest," said Dr. Agrawal. "Nobody really gave her a chance of coming back. Somehow she managed to get revived again. Everybody was very surprised."

Then Falak underwent a further operation: the insertion of a tube into her trachea to assist her breathing.

EXCERPTS FROM OPERATION NOTE. DATE OF SURGERY: JAN. 23, 2012. TRACHEOSTOMY UNDER GA

POSITION: THE PATIENT IS POSITIONED WITH THE NECK EXTENDED, WITH A ROLL OF CLOTH BETWEEN THE SHOULDER BLADES AND THE HEAD IN A HEAD RING.

INCISION: 1 CM INCISION MADE VERTICALLY WITH
A SCALPEL, BETWEEN THE SECOND AND THIRD
TRACHEAL RINGS.

Back in the ICU, in a full-size bed, Falak was attended round the clock by a team of nurses.

They gave her sponge baths. They wrapped her in a hypothermic blanket to treat her hypothermia. They suctioned secretions through the trachea tube every two hours. They fed her a high-protein diet that included raw eggs, milk and supplements. They gave her antibiotics and other medicines by injection and drip. They monitored her heart rate, her breathing, the oxygen level in her blood and her blood pressure. They changed her diapers. Every four hours, they rubbed her limbs with coconut oil to stimulate her circulation and lubricate her skin. Even among a crew used to dealing with broken bodies, the unconscious, parentless, beaten-up baby drew the nurses to her.

"Our relationship was simply like mother," says Chetna Malhotra, one of the team. She would whisper in the infant's ear, "Get well soon, Falak. Don't worry. We are there for you." Another, Sheenamol Bejoi, held her cell phone to Falak's ear so she could hear music Ms. Bejoi had downloaded.

But the mystery of who Falak was, whom she belonged to, and what had befallen her was no closer to being solved. Gudiya, who had brought Falak to the trauma center, knew little of the baby's past. The police had few leads, and showed little interest in the case, Dr. Agrawal says. A police official in charge of the investigation declined comment.

As Dr. Agrawal monitored the baby's knife-edge condition, somewhere in the back of his mind the absence of information began to bother him. He thought about his own 6-year-old daughter. He thought about what it would take to beat up a child so severely. And he thought,

"We might never know who she is."

On January 25, 2012, one week after Falak was admitted, the doctor began his rounds promptly at 8:00 A.M.

Dr. Agrawal is of medium build with conservatively cut hair. He wears glasses, a white coat and comfortable shoes. He is friendly but not effusive. And he does long rounds.

That day, he visited patients for three or four hours, a large contingent of residents and nurses following behind him. Along the way, Dr. Agrawal pointed out bits and pieces he thought could have been done better. Toward the end, in the ICU, he reached Falak's bedside. The bite marks on her cheeks stood out, as if he were seeing them for the first time.

"What's the status now? Have you found out anything?" he asked the team. Have the police come? Is there any more information on who is looking after the kid? The answer each time was no.

"What's going on?" Dr. Agrawal asked, his voice rising. "Is nobody interested? We are part of society here.

What kind of doctors and nurses are we? Why aren't you all as anxious as I am about this kid, huh?"

Silence.

"We, too, were helpless because we ourselves can't go out and find out about the history of the patients," said Avijit Sarkari, a trainee neurosurgeon who was there. "But yes, we remained silent to his questions that morning."

With an uncharacteristically dramatic flourish, Dr. Agrawal took out his phone and declared, "I am going to call up the media, okay? Maybe that's the only way we're going to get to the bottom of it, because you people are not at all interested in finding out."

He knew many of the Delhi media's health reporters. The first to spring to mind was Rhythma Kaul at the *Hindustan Times*, an English-language daily.

Dr. Agrawal would say later that he regretted making the call as soon as he hung up the phone, because of the maelstrom it provoked. But at the time, with his medical team of about 20 crowded around, he said simply, "Rhythma, I might have a story for you."

◆

Rhythma Kaul was covering a school deworming initiative when Dr. Agrawal called. He described Falak's condition, dwelling on the human bite marks.

Dr. Agrawal says he was chiefly interested in having Ms. Kaul make inquiries that would put pressure on the police to speed up their investigation. He called it "a little bit of social work."

Ms. Kaul, 29 years old, took a photographer with her to the hospital to check out what the doctor had told her, then returned to the office to try to make a story from what little she knew.

It was the day before Republic Day, a commemoration of the founding of modern India. It is marked with an early-morning military parade on Rajpath, the avenue that bisects the sweeping grassy mall between Rashtrapati Bhavan, the president's palace, and the India Gate arch in the center of New Delhi.

A story on the parade preparations was a natural lead for the next day's paper. But there was shock value in the plight of a battered, abandoned baby girl on a day that celebrates India's achievements.

"The editors got excited by the fact that we didn't know from where the baby had come but it had been ritually battered," Ms. Kaul said in an interview. "They thought they should take it up as a cause. A girl child on Republic Day and this was the state of the girl child in our country."

Perhaps, Ms. Kaul and others thought, someone had tried to kill Falak but failed. By early evening, colleagues were whispering to Ms. Kaul that her story had front-page potential.

At home that night, Dr. Agrawal says he told his wife about calling a reporter from the ICU and that he regretted it. But since he hadn't heard back from Ms. Kaul, he thought there might not be a story.

"You are like this only; you do things and think later," his wife told him, he says. But she also said, "Okay, whatever's going to happen happened. You did the right thing. You felt so strongly about the baby."

The next morning, at around 6:45, Ms. Kaul's father woke his daughter at their family home with a copy of the paper. The headline plastered across the top read: ABANDONED, 2-YR-OLD BATTLES FOR LIFE IN ICU.

The photo, taken from above, showed a small baby lying on a large bed. Falak was not named.

"I'm proud of you," her father told Ms. Kaul. "This is your career best so far."

Dr. Agrawal, an early riser, was at his house on an off-duty day when the paper landed on his doorstep at about 7:30. "The first thing I felt was dread, because I thought 'My God, nobody in my center knows about this,'" he said.

Soon his phone was buzzing with calls from other reporters. The hospital staff also were besieged with calls—and caught unawares. The trauma center's head administrator, Mahesh Chandra Misra, didn't even know who Falak was: she hadn't stood out enough among the center's 170 patients for him to be notified.

Scrambling on a public holiday, hospital officials arranged a press conference so reporters could be given what information the hospital had at the same time. The big Hindi- and English-language 24-hour television news channels sent broadcast vans and cameras. Suddenly Falak's touch-and-go condition was being monitored on live television, putting the hospital on edge.

When Ms. Kaul telephoned one trauma center official, she says she was told, "Haven't you done enough damage already?"

No one from the hospital called Dr. Agrawal.

The story of Baby Falak, soon dubbed "India's Baby," handily eclipsed the Republic Day parade.

"How could anyone bludgeon, bite and all but kill a two-year-old infant?" declared Vishnu Som, an anchor for news channel NDTV, at the start of a bulletin. "That's what people in the national capital want to know after news broke about a horrific assault that left a child brain damaged and fighting for her life."

Barkha Dutt, group editor for the channel, said in an interview that it was highly unusual for a story about a child in distress to gain so much attention.

"I would say it was a nine out of ten story, that's what made it unusual. It was the top story"—not political parties, foreign policy, terrorism, a rich person's wedding or the Indian Premier League cricket. "Such stories are rarely given the primacy of hard news."

◆

The round-the-clock media attention made Falak's plight a public spectacle. Delhi's Child Welfare Committee objected to photos of Falak being broadcast.

Falak's surgeons faced quizzing from reporters and second-guessing from colleagues about their treatment of the baby. They gave daily press conferences that provided the latest on her care and condition—which was then duly disseminated to the nation. Live coverage of medical bulletins usually is reserved for ailing senior politicians or terrorist attacks.

The furor strained Dr. Agrawal's relationship with his boss, Dr. Misra, the trauma center's chief. Only on January 29, three days after the story broke, did Dr. Agrawal appear before reporters for the first time.

Afterward, he caught up with Dr. Misra as they walked on the concrete ramp outside the center's main entrance.

"Sir, I am very sorry about this whole thing coming out in the paper without information," Dr. Agrawal said.

"Deepak," responded Dr. Misra. "You should have at least told me."

"I know, sir," Dr. Agrawal said. "I am sorry." With that, the two men moved on.

At the trauma center, some followed every turn in the news. Others wondered why the media was making such a big deal about Falak, given the number of babies who suffer and die in India every year.

Outside and around the world, Falak's helplessness triggered a passionate, personal response, which reached Dr. Agrawal in waves of e-mails.

[These excerpts have been lightly edited.]

Dear Dr. Deepak,

I was in dilemma about sending this mail to you. At last, I firmly felt that I should send it to you.

Whole nation is eagerly waiting to listen that Falak regains her consciousness. I am confident that success in this regard is destined for you and your team.

Since you are leading a team of doctors attending Falak and the situation is becoming clear to you day by day, still I would genuinely request your nurses to murmur positively whenever they are attending Falak.

By the way, is there any good news of Falak for us?

Hi Dr. Deepak,

I wish to express my thanks and gratitude for the efforts taken in helping baby falak getting a fighting chance to live.

We are an Indian couple staying in Australia and trying to have a child of our own. It has been 7 years but we haven't been blessed with a child.

We were considering of adopting baby Falak if we are given this opportunity.

We are more than confident of our ability to provide for the child and work in her best interest.

Regards,

Sir,

Hope you are fine. May GOD show you the right way.
Sir, I pray for Baby Falak.
May ALLAH shower HIS MAGIC here.

I dont know what exactly to say . . .

I know this—I am sad . . . weeping for falak.

I am a mother of 2 kids. I am in Dubai.

One student from Central Asia who was attending a local university walked into the trauma center and said, according to Dr. Agrawal, "I want to look at the baby. I feel that if I just stand there and give her my energy, she will get better."

Dr. Agrawal refused to allow her into the ICU. But she kept pleading, and waited for four hours.

"Okay, fine," he said. "You go and have a look." Accompanied by a nurse, the woman entered the ICU and stood by Falak's bed for 10 minutes.

She asked to come back again; Dr. Agrawal asked her not to. But the woman returned with a card and a teddy bear, Dr. Agrawal says.

"You please put it in front of her," she told Dr. Agrawal. He says he refused. She pleaded. Once again, he relented. The staff hung the two-foot-long pink bear on Falak's intravenous drip stand. The baby's eyes were open, but she could not fix her gaze.

Painting of a cross on the wall of a Pachwara house.
(Paul Beckett/The Wall Street Journal)

ABOVE: The village of Pachwara. *(Paul Beckett/ The Wall Street Journal)*

LEFT: Sister Valsa John Malamel *(Courtesy of the Malamel Family)*

FACING PAGE, TOP: Compound of a Pachwara house where Sister Valsa lived. *(Paul Beckett/The Wall Street Journal)*

FACING PAGE, RIGHT: Binej Hembrom is the traditional head of 32 tribal villages including Pachwara. *(Krishna Pokharel/The Wall Street Journal)*

ABOVE: A site of mining near Pachwara. *(Krishna Pokharel/The Wall Street Journal)*

BELOW: A girl collects nuggets of coal on the roadside near Pachwara. *(Krishna Pokharel/The Wall Street Journal)*

ABOVE: The entrance to Sister Valsa's rooms. *(Krishna Pokharel/The Wall Street Journal)*

BELOW: Sister Valsa's grave in a Christian public cemetery in Dumka, about two hours' drive from Pachwara, where she lived. *(Paul Beckett/The Wall Street Journal)*

Surajmuni Hembrom in the twilight in Pachwara.
(Paul Beckett/The Wall Street Journal)

ABOVE: The scene at the New Delhi Railway Station. *(Sanjit Das/Panos for The Wall Street Journal)*

BELOW: A woman with a child at a New Delhi train station. *(Sanjit Das/Panos for The Wall Street Journal)*

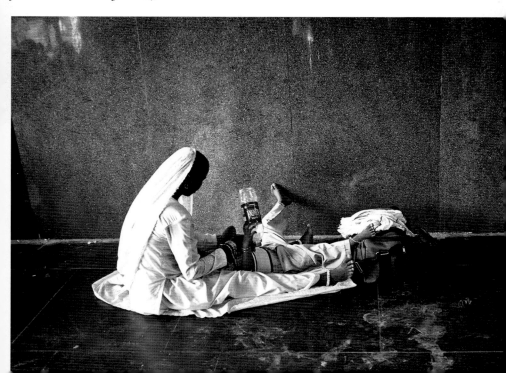

ABOVE: Munni Khatoon in May 2012. *(Krishna Pokharel/The Wall Street Journal)*

BELOW: The metro train station at Delhi's Uttam Nagar. *(Sanjit Das/Panos for The Wall Street Journal)*

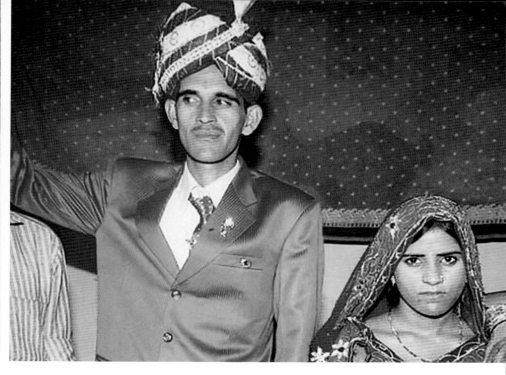

ABOVE: Harpal Singh and Munni Khatoon. *(Photo: Singh Family)*

BELOW: The entrance to a temple at Delhi's Govindpuri area. *(Sanjit Das/Panos for The Wall Street Journal)*

ABOVE: The Mahipalpur area near the Delhi airport. *(Sanjit Das/Panos for The Wall Street Journal)*

BELOW: The intensive care unit at the AIIMS trauma center. *(Sanjit Das/Panos for The Wall Street Journal)*

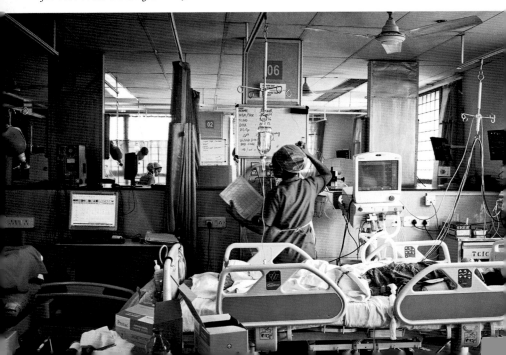

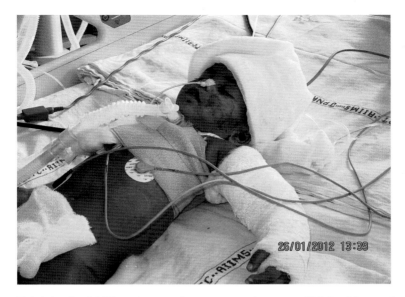

ABOVE: Falak in the ICU. *(Courtesy of the All India Institute of Medical Sciences)*

BELOW: The grave of Falak. *(Sanjit Das/Panos for The Wall Street Journal)*

LEFT: A January 6, 2013, memorial for the gang-rape victim in New Delhi. (*Mail Today/Zuma Press*)

BELOW: Passersby near the spot where the two victims were dumped, naked and bleeding, by the side of the road. (*Tripti Lahiri/The Wall Street Journal*)

OPPOSITE PAGE, TOP: Her last gift to him was a gray tie. It remains in an envelope in his New Delhi apartment. "I tried to do things that made her happy." (*Manpreet Romana/The Wall Street Journal*)

OPPOSITE PAGE, BOTTOM: Ravi Dass slum, where several of the accused live, sits by an ancient monument in Delhi. (*Amol Sharma/The Wall Street Journal*)

ABOVE: Indians hold a candlelight vigil on December 30, 2012, in New Delhi in memory of the victim of gang rape on a Delhi bus. *(Associated Press/AP Photo/ Saurabh Das)*

BELOW: An anti-rape protestor chants slogans as she braces herself against the spray fired from police water canons in front of Delhi's India Gate on December 23, 2012. *(Getty Images)*

LEFT: An Indian girl holds a placard as she attends a protest rally on January 15, 2013, in Delhi. *(EPA/Harish Tyagi)*

BELOW: Remnants of the candlelight vigil on January 3, 2013, in memory of the 23-year-old Delhi gang-rape victim. *(Associated Press)*

ABOVE: A police officer cleared traffic at the New Delhi district court on January 7, 2013, to make way for a police van believed to be carrying the five men accused in the attack. *(Associated Press)*

BELOW: A map of India detailing statistics of sexual assaults against women in 2011, including reported rapes and conviction rates of rape cases. *(WSJ Research)*

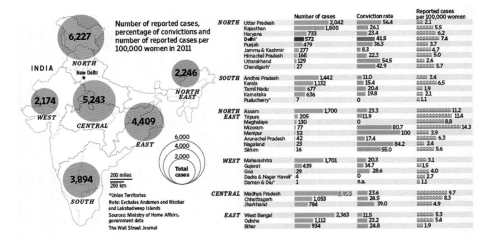

Number of reported cases, percentage of convictions and number of reported cases per 100,000 women in 2011

		Number of cases	Conviction rate	Reported cases per 100,000 women
NORTH	Uttar Pradesh	2,042	56.4	2.1
	Rajasthan	1,800	26.1	5.5
	Haryana	733	23.4	6.2
	Delhi*	572	41.5	7.4
	Punjab	479	36.3	3.7
	Jammu & Kashmir	277	8.3	4.7
	Himachal Pradesh	168	22.3	5.0
	Uttarakhand	129	54.5	2.6
	Chandigarh*	27	42.9	5.7
SOUTH	Andhra Pradesh	1,442	11.0	3.4
	Kerala	1,132	15.4	6.5
	Tamil Nadu	677	20.4	1.9
	Karnataka	636	19.8	2.1
	Puducherry*	7	0	1.1
NORTH EAST	Assam	1,700	23.3	11.2
	Tripura	205	11.9	11.4
	Meghalaya	130	0	8.8
	Mizoram	77	80.7	14.3
	Manipur	53	100	3.9
	Arunachal Pradesh	42	17.4	6.3
	Nagaland	23	84.2	2.4
	Sikkim	16	55.0	5.6
WEST	Maharashtra	1,701	20.3	3.1
	Gujarat	439	14.7	1.5
	Goa	29	28.6	4.0
	Dadra & Nagar Haveli*	4	0	2.7
	Daman & Diu*	1	n.a.	1.1
CENTRAL	Madhya Pradesh	3,406	23.6	9.7
	Chhattisgarh	1,053	24.5	8.3
	Jharkhand	784	39.0	4.9
EAST	West Bengal	2,363	11.5	5.3
	Odisha	1,112	23.2	5.4
	Bihar	934	24.8	1.9

INDIA 6,227
NORTH 5,243
New Delhi
NORTH EAST 2,246
WEST 2,174
CENTRAL 4,409
EAST
SOUTH 3,894

6,000 / 4,000 / 2,000 Total cases

200 miles
200 km

*Union Territories
Note: Excludes Andaman and Nicobar and Lakshadweep Islands
Sources: Ministry of Home Affairs, government data
The Wall Street Journal

6

The Radiant Sky

The frenetic media attention—outraged talk shows, crime-scene documentaries, heartfelt commentaries, and prodding public statements from Delhi's child protection authorities—upped the tempo of the police investigation into the battered baby girl lying in a Delhi trauma center.

A group of officers fanned out across the country to piece together the puzzle: Who was Falak and how had she gotten there?

On January 27, 2012, a crime team from a local police station photographed and seized room 210 at the Shalimar PG guesthouse near the airport, where the baby had stayed. They logged a bloodstained coverless pillow from the room's double bed, according to police records.

Three days later, officials from the Central Forensic Science Laboratory at the Central Bureau of Investigation, at the request of Delhi police, took evidence from a blood stain on the room's western wall, a blood stain on the bathroom wall and two pieces of bloodstained cotton wool. They also removed 35 items of baby clothing, police records show.

Over the next few weeks, the cops rounded up about a dozen people, the arrests heralded in press releases. "Sincere efforts of the teams yielded results," one of them read.

◆

Laxmi Devi, the woman who said in her confession to police that she was part of the plan to lure Falak's mother to Delhi, was charged with crimes related to abandoning a child under the age of 12, compelling a woman into marriage, cheating, criminal conspiracy and cruelty to a juvenile. She denied the charges.

Pratima Devi Chatterjee, the cook who looked after Falak when the baby first arrived in Delhi, was charged with child-related crimes. She denied the charges. She would be part of the same trial as Laxmi Devi.

Police were searching for several people. They included Shankar, the man who first approached Falak's mother in Bihar; Saroj Chaudhary, who was accused by Falak's mother of conspiring in the Rajasthan marriage ruse; and Manoj Kumar Nandan, the odd-job man who was instrumental in passing along both Falak and her older brother, Golu. Police listed those three as suspects. Neither they nor their lawyers could be reached.

Munni Khatoon, Falak's mother, was found by police at her new home in Jhunjhunu. Neither she nor her husband had told the community that she wasn't who she said she was, they both say.

But even before the police arrived, gossip had reached Mr. Singh's mother that her new daughter-in-law was a Muslim with children, and she confronted her son. Afterward, Mr. Singh's mother purchased a suitcase of clothes for Ms. Khatoon and told her she would have to leave, both women say.

Mr. Singh's brother planned to take her to Delhi on February 4. The police arrived from Delhi first and took Ms. Khatoon into custody. Before Ms. Khatoon left, Mr. Singh told her, "Go back to your kids, and whenever you need any help from me, I can help you."

After that, Mr. Singh says he grew a two-inch beard to be less recognizable in his community. He later spent time at an ashram in Delhi run by the spiritual leader whom members of his family follow.

Mr. Singh petitioned the local council to force his cousin, Amar, to return money he says he was cheated out of at the wedding. Amar Singh denies selling Ms. Khatoon or cheating his cousin. He would later testify that he, like Harpal Singh, was misguided by Saroj Chaudhary and others about Ms. Khatoon's true identity.

Ms. Khatoon was taken to a women's shelter in Delhi. One day, she visited her daughter in the intensive care unit. "I was hit by a big blow of regret and guilty feelings to see my little baby in that condition," she said. She says she couldn't face returning.

Ms. Khatoon's 4-year-old daughter, Khusboo, was traced to Muzaffarpur in Bihar and brought to Delhi.

Police found Khatoon's 5-year-old son, Golu, at the home of Mohammed Sakil and his family in Delhi's Uttam Nagar neighborhood. The family already knew the connection. When a news bulletin about Falak had appeared on television the night before the police arrived, Mr. Sakil declared to the family that the boy was the baby's brother.

"I still have a feeling that he will come back," Mr. Sakil's wife said of Golu. "I loved him a lot."

Pooja and Sandeep Pandey, the couple who allegedly gave 14-year-old Gudiya the choice of marriage or prostitution, were arrested and charged with a range of crimes, including gang rape, earning from prostitution and inducing a person into prostitution. The other couple whom Gudiya said she worked for at that time face similar charges. All deny the charges, their lawyers say. Their trial has yet to begin.

Mohammed Dilshad, also known as Rajkumar, the taxi driver who took tiny Sania and named her Falak, was arrested and charged with a series of child- and prostitution-related crimes. He denies the charges.

He is part of two separate trials, one concerning what allegedly happened to Gudiya; the other on what allegedly happened to Falak. The latter has yet to begin; the former is nearly completed.

"I was just trying to save a girl who was in the clutch of prostitution and had adopted an abandoned baby as my own daughter," his lawyer says his client told him. "What crime did I commit by just trying to help them?"

Gudiya was placed under the supervision of Delhi's Child Welfare Committee. At one hearing, her father, Jitender Gupta, was also present. When he suggested that he had looked after his daughter in the past, she became irate.

"How much you took care of me?" she shouted at him, according to an official who was present. Of her placement in an orphanage, she said, "You had to do that, even if you are alive? You had to say that I have no father?"

Mr. Gupta said in an interview that officials coerced his daughter into making those statements. A lawyer for her declined comment.

Gudiya told the authorities what she knew about the prostitution ring she says she was part of, according to a counseling report. She told them about a man known as "Big Boss" who "takes young and slim girls to work for him." And she talked about hotels in Mahipalpur, the district by the airport where she and Falak stayed, where young girls were known to be farmed out for paid sex.

◆

As the story unfolded and the police sweep took place, India's child protection network came under scrutiny.

The Juvenile Justice (Care and Protection of Children) Act of 2000 established child welfare committees that work with children who need protection and help rehabilitate them. A separate Juvenile Justice Board deals with children who are in conflict with the law.

Another initiative, called the Integrated Child Protection Scheme, aims to provide a safety net for children at risk by tying together nongovernmental organizations, local officials (right down to the village level) and others who can spot and intervene in cases where they think children may be vulnerable.

In Falak's case, Delhi's Child Welfare Committee became closely involved after Gudiya and the baby arrived at AIIMS. The city's Juvenile Justice Board is also holding hearings on what happened. But, several experts say, many child protection authorities in India aren't functioning effectively and fail to identify children at risk.

Falak's predicament "one hundred percent could have been prevented," said Parveen Amanullah, Bihar's social welfare minister, in an interview.

Ms. Amanullah says her state, one of India's poorest, is "just starting and we are learning" about what needs to be done to better protect children. "Our system is totally un-sensitive," she acknowledged. She added that combating human trafficking is not high on either her government's or the public's agenda. "The general public is not even bothered about it," she said.

◆

Deepak Agrawal, the neurosurgeon charged with Falak's care, has a simple way of rating your chances of survival in life. If you are vertical, they are high. As soon as you are horizontal, they plummet. He means this literally.

So it was with Falak. Her lengthening stay lying flat in a hospital bed made her vulnerable to a chest infection, a brain infection and septicemia. She was plied with antibiotics.

Whether a patient survives such an onslaught of infection depends on what Dr. Agrawal, after saying he has no words to describe it, calls "the drive to survive." It is the inexplicable something whereby an individual's brain and the body's chemicals interact in a way that no one understands but that makes the difference between life and death.

"She had a roller-coaster ride" in her first weeks in hospital, he said of Falak.

The more weeks that passed, the more those around Falak connected with her.

Rhythma Kaul, the *Hindustan Times* reporter who first wrote about the baby, says she considered adopting her—until Dr. Agrawal told her that even if Falak survived and left the hospital, she would need constant care and would have a severely impaired quality of life because of the damage to her brain. Ms. Kaul, who works from mid-morning to late in the evening, knew she wasn't in a position to take on that role.

Mahesh Chandra Misra, the trauma center's chief, says he noticed what he considered promising signs of growing awareness in the child: when visitors approached, her heart beat, registered on the monitor beside her bed, increased to 130 or 140 beats a minute.

The nurses caring for Falak saw her heightened heart rate differently: as a sign of anxiety near strangers. They prided themselves on the fact that when they were around, her heartbeat remained constant at 90.

On February 20, 2012, Falak needed another operation: the installation of a shunt to drain fluid from her brain. She pulled through again, and gradually her condition improved.

The media coverage was intense. "The most compelling phase was when the baby was struggling to make it; it was the point of maximum engagement," said Barkha Dutt at NDTV. Some people transferred their fears and vulnerability onto the baby and gained confidence with every sign of her improving health, she says. Others saw a stark image of a destitute child from which they could not turn away.

In early March, Dr. Agrawal recommended that Falak be moved out of the intensive care unit and into a regular ward for monitoring.

When the ICU nurses heard about this, they asked Dr. Agrawal if they could continue to care for Falak, even though she would be out of their area. It was an extraordinary request given that the ICU already was short-staffed. But the sister in charge says she realized how attached the nurses had become to the baby, and agreed.

Falak got better and better. There was talk in the hospital of her being discharged if the appropriate home could be found—talk that was quickly picked up by the press.

Munni Khatoon says women in her shelter who were following the story told her, "Your baby is fine now. The doctors have taken her out of the ICU and they are planning to release her soon."

So when police asked her to go get her child, she was elated. "I thought she has gotten well and I can bring her with me," she said.

Instead, a female police inspector broke the news that Falak had died.

EXCERPTS FROM INTERNATIONAL MEDICAL CERTIFICATE OF CAUSE OF DEATH

DATE & TIME OF DEATH: 03/15/2012 21:40

CAUSE OF DEATH: CARDIAC ARRHYTHMIAS

ANTECEDENT CAUSES: SEPTICEMIA WITH PNEUMONITIS WITH MENINGITIS

MORBID CONDITIONS: SEVERE HEAD INJURY WITH POLYTRAUMA

Dr. Agrawal was at home, having skipped out early from a dinner that followed a course he attended that day called "Doctors as Leaders." He got the call from the resident doctor in Falak's ward.

"I felt really, really sad that time, especially because I had thought we had gone over the worst," Dr. Agrawal said. His mind started to rationalize it to compensate: "Maybe that's the best for her because she's undergone so much."

Television channels bombarded him with requests for a few words in front of an outside broadcast van. "I am not interested," he told them.

Rhythma Kaul says she felt grief. She had become so closely associated with the child that her colleagues would ask her daily, "How's the baby?"

"It was like she was my baby almost," Ms. Kaul said. But knowing what kind of impaired existence Falak would have had in life, she added, "I think it's for her good that she died. She's gone to a better world, I hope."

The nurses who had looked after Falak pinned a sign on the ward's notice board. It read:

A TRIBUTE TO BABY FALAK

You were to us more than a patient. you evoked the feelings of parents. your cries and cooes were a tickle to our hearts. How we loved you dear Falak! But now we know that the god who formed you and let you into our hands loves you more. we miss you

Let your soul rest in peace . . .

Falak died five days shy of her second birthday. In an order soon after, Delhi's Child Welfare Committee said, "The story of this child is a grim reminder of the failure of the government to put the child protection mechanism in place. There are *lakhs* [hundreds of thousands] of Falaks in our country who are waiting for immediate help."

Falak's death was front-page news. But the media quickly moved on to other stories: the annual presentation of the budget in Parliament, the resignation of the railways minister.

"After the baby died, the story died," said Ms. Kaul. Still, all the attention had spurred the investigation into tracking down many of those allegedly involved before Falak passed away.

Since then, "Baby Falak" has become shorthand for cases of battered babies in India, especially for girls unwanted by their parents. And such stories have risen in the news pecking order.

A BABY FALAK IN BANGALORE, 3-MONTH-OLD GIRL BAT-TLING FOR LIFE, read an April 2012 headline on IBNLive, the website of the CNN-IBN news channel, above a story about a baby in Bangalore whose father allegedly tortured her because he "was not happy with delivery of a girl."

ANOTHER BABY FALAK? INFANT FOUND ABANDONED IN DHAMNOD, read the *Daily Bhaskar* newspaper on May 30, when a 10-month-old girl was found at a roadside in the central Indian state of Madhya Pradesh.

A few days later, NDTV reported on an 18-month-old baby admitted to hospital in the city of Indore with signs of abuse under the headline: "INDORE'S BABY FALAK: CIGARETTE BURNS, MULTIPLE FRACTURES."

◆

For a few months after Falak's death, Munni Khatoon lived in cramped quarters with one of her brothers in West Delhi.

One afternoon, Golu, her 5-year-old son, said, "Sania has died now. A cycle hit her and she died."

"Yes, a big cycle," Khusboo, his sister, chimed in.

Ms. Khatoon speaks reservedly, rarely making eye contact. "As a good mother, I shouldn't have left her and the other kids alone even for a single day," she said of her youngest. "Now, after all that happened, I have no confidence in myself and I doubt every step I take."

But at times, Khatoon shows signs of moving on. She likes to lock the door to her room and put on jeans and a shirt, something women in her village don't wear. She sings to herself—Bollywood numbers about betrayal and separation.

Initially, through her brother, she got part-time work at a fan repair shop. Recently, the Child Welfare Committee arranged for the government to hire her in a children's home for 6-to-10-year-olds in Lajpat Nagar, a neighborhood in South Delhi.

She expects to earn about 7,000 rupees ($130) a month as a "house auntie," a caretaker; her children can live there with her for free.

She does not want to return to her village or to reunite with Shah Hussain, the father of her three children. Mr. Hussain says he doesn't want to get back together either, but he will if his community demands it. In their village of Maripur, in Bihar, there is friction between their two families, according to both sides.

One evening, Ms. Khatoon's father called her brother's place. Ms. Khatoon talked to him. They were both in tears.

"Abba," she says she told him, "I did a mistake by not listening to you and marrying Shah Hussain. Please forgive me."

"Okay, I forgive you," he replied. "But now live your life properly and stay with your other kids in Delhi."

◆

One side of the broad avenue that connects New Delhi to Old Delhi houses India's Fleet Street, a short strip piled high with the offices of some of the nation's biggest newspapers.

Off a dirty lane full of parked cars behind *The Indian Express*, a quiet pathway leads to a cemetery. Through the gates, about 30 meters from a small mosque, close to the right side of the path, is a piece of unmarked sandstone about 18 inches high.

The grave beneath it is three feet deep, one foot wide and three and a half feet long. It is overshadowed by higher headstones and a tree.

Falak is buried here, covered by a pile of dirt caked into a mound. One day, two children were selling bottles of water to be poured over the mud in what they claimed was a traditional ritual.

Falak was brought to the cemetery by a small group of policemen at 4:00 P.M. on March 16, 2012. They handed her to the imam's wife, a 65-year-old woman named Samina. She washes the corpses of children brought to the grave-yard, about four or five a month.

She took Falak to an enclosed area, about six feet across, where her family usually washes in private. Its walls are made from branches, a tarpaulin, laundry lines hanging with blankets and mats, and two crumbling doors. Inside the enclosure, paving stones and concrete form a slope that ends in a small basin of mud.

Samina was joined that day by Munni Khatoon. Falak was placed on a small bed. Ms. Khatoon poured the water as Samina washed the baby with Lux soap, taking care not to open the stitches that covered her skull, chest and legs. She also rubbed the body with scented oil. Ms. Khatoon wailed.

Samina prompted Ms. Khatoon that it is customary to say three times, "My Lord gave to me and I give to you."

"How can I say this? I'm not in a condition to say this," Ms. Khatoon cried.

"Do it fast; we have to go," the cops interrupted, according to Samina.

Eventually, Ms. Khatoon got the words out. "I forced her to do it," Samina said. The baby was dressed in five pieces of white cotton. Then Falak was carried away for burial.

There were about 10 people around the grave: Ms. Khatoon; the imam; the police; and a few journalists, who took pictures. Wives of some of the cemetery workers hung around. They had heard about Falak's case from television.

The imam read from the Koran. The ceremony lasted about 90 minutes. Ms. Khatoon cried throughout.

Afterward, when the death was recorded in the cemetery's records, written in Urdu on a rectangular piece of paper, the baby's name, as stated by her mother, was written as Sania Falak. One way to translate it: "Radiant Sky."

Epilogue

A Nurse's Tribute to Baby Falak

There were several memorable aspects about reporting the Baby Falak story that ran on *WSJ*'s blog *India Real Time*. Among the revelations, for us, was the high level of dedication shown for the tiny girl by staff at the trauma center of the All India Institute of Medical Sciences. India's government-run hospitals, for good reason, are often criticized for being substandard, lacking in crucial resources and competent staff. But in this case, the efforts of the doctors and nurses in caring for Sania Khatoon, the baby who became known as Falak, was impressive, especially the willingness of her nurses to go beyond the to-do list of their duties and invest themselves in the baby's care. We tried to reflect that in the piece and, after it ran, one of Falak's nurses, Chetna Malhotra, penned a poem in tribute to the baby. We are reproducing it here, translated from Hindi.

In Memory of Falak

BY CHETNA MALHOTRA

Whose body was as tender as a flower
But darkness had seized her life
Innocence expressed itself on her face
Yes, yes, that angel's name was baby Falak!

What did she get in her life?
Neither her parents' company
Nor the care of somebody to call her own
Childhood for her became a curse
She became the victim of poverty and helplessness.

Neither she got the warmth of her mother
Nor did she get her father's support
And nor could she spend time with her brother and
sister.

I wonder what lines had made home on her palms
I wonder what destiny had decorated her forehead
Oh, what a cobweb of existence this little angel had
to be in?
She went through so much suffering that would
shake our soul.

On her face filled with innocence
Were inflicted the marks of devilishness
And her body was given several wounds
And from each wound, her life would bleed.

She had learned groaning
At the age of laughing
She made all the pains her own
By forgetting the game of childhood.

But her courage was undying
She fought with all her life
She got the love from the strangers
She had the prayers of people from all over the world.

But one day she lost
To the maze of this life
To the inhumane humans
And to their acts.

But as she was going away
She showed to us the face of the bad
And she went away by giving us this deep thought
"What will happen to us?"

"Will the childhood die like this
In the maze of helplessness and greed?
Will the woman keep on being sold
By the hands of devils?"

MISS U FALAK . . .

What Is Sacrosanct

Munni Khatoon, mother of "Baby Falak," now stays at the government-run children's home in South Delhi where she works as a house caretaker.

Her two other kids, Golu and Khusboo, stay with her and study at a nearby school.

Ms. Khatoon occasionally visits her brother's family in West Delhi on weekends. She says she doesn't plan to return to her husband and the father of her kids, Shah Hussain. The couple is not yet considered separated under Islamic law on marriage.

"It's good for the future of my two kids that I stay and work here," Ms. Khatoon said in a recent conversation.

In late June 2012, police arrested Mr. Hussain at the roadside tire repair shop in the Delhi suburb of Gurgaon, where he worked. He now faces trial in Bihar on charges he raped a girl in 2010, which he denies.

A police officer in charge of investigation of the case said Mr. Hussain is out on bail after spending some time in jail.

Some people in Mr. Hussain's village of Maripur said he now works at an apparel business in Mumbai. He couldn't be reached for comment.

◆

Harpal Singh, the farmer in Rajasthan who was duped into marrying Ms. Khatoon, said he has yet to find a new bride. "It's not that easy that you find a girl today and marry her tomorrow," he said.

Gudiya, the teenager who cared for Falak and brought her to the hospital, is at a juvenile rehabilitation home in Delhi.

The trial of three key people involved in the Baby Falak affair who were charged with child- and prostitution-related crimes—Laxmi Devi, Saroj Chaudhary, Mohammed Dilshad—is nearing completion at a district court in Delhi, lawyers and police say. Pratima Devi Chatterjee and Manoj Kumar Nandan, both of whom were charged with child-related crimes, are part of the same trial. Mr. Dilshad continues to be held in jail while others are out on bail. The accused deny any wrongdoing.

A separate trial of the six people—including Mr. Dilshad, Sandeep Pandey and his wife, Pooja—who were allegedly involved in the sexual exploitation of Gudiya has been delayed because of the transfer of judges hearing the case, according to police and the lawyers involved. Police also have added Jitender Gupta, Gudiya's father, with behaving cruelly toward his teenage daughter, which is a crime under India's juvenile-protection laws. He denies the charge. He is currently out on bail.

Shankar—the man whom Ms. Khatoon said laid the trap that lured her to Delhi—is still on the run, according to police.

◆

Deepak Agrawal, the neurosurgeon who was in charge of the treatment of Falak at the trauma center of the All India Institute of Medical Sciences in Delhi, said he hasn't come across another case of a battered baby girl. But he said he has noticed a groundswell of public debate and discussion on the issues of women and children in India since Falak's story dominated national media in the early months of 2012.

"In retrospect, the story of Baby Falak marked a defining point for the evolution of Indian society, because for the first time in my life I am seeing people talking about these issues seriously," Dr. Agrawal said.

Dr. Agrawal said his professional involvement in the care of Baby Falak made him hold sacrosanct the minimum of one hour he spends with his daughter every day.

"We hope that by the time of our children, the society will be more equal for both genders," he said.

PART III

The Delhi Bus Rape

A gang rape that took place on the night of December 16, 2012, in Delhi, India's capital, shocked the world.

In part, it was because the crime itself had the elements of a horror movie. A young woman and her male friend board a bus where the only passengers, five young men and a teenage boy, appear normal. But then the lights are turned out and the attack begins.

The incident sparked widespread outrage and demonstrations against public authorities. It prompted a review of India's laws to prevent crimes against women.

Most movingly, it was a tragedy played out on a small stage, involving a bright 23-year-old student, her poor but striving family, her relationship with a higher-caste male friend—and those who tore it all apart.

The Wall Street Journal wrote the following exclusive stories from January to March 2013 based on extensive interviews with the young woman's friends, family members, officials involved in the investigation, and those who knew the men charged with the crime. And it used the incident to look more broadly at the ways in which the relationship between the sexes in India is broken.

1

The Victim

BY KRISHNA POKHAREL AND SAURABH CHATURVEDI IN
GORAKHPUR, INDIA; VIBHUTI AGARWAL IN DEHRADUN; AND TRIPTI
LAHIRI IN DELHI

It was early afternoon just before Christmas in India's capital, and a young woman spoke to her friend on the phone, eager to get together.

"Wake up, wake up," she told him. "It's already very late—one o'clock."

The two agreed to meet. And so began an innocent outing that set in motion a killing that would horrify the world.

The two met at Select Citywalk, a trendy mall where Delhi's 20-somethings gather to spend pocket change and enjoy a small taste of the glamour promised by India's economic rise. The young woman—her family's nickname for her was Bitiya, which means "daughter"—admired a long coat in a shop window, her friend says in an interview. He thought he would like to buy it for her later. Then they took in a movie, *Life of Pi*, sitting in the same seats where, on an earlier visit, they had watched *Gulliver's Travels* together.

A few hours later, the pair were dumped, naked and bleeding, from a private bus along a highway. Both had been viciously attacked with an iron rod, according to police, and the young woman so violently raped that she died two weeks later, on December 29.

Her death spawned a moment of national introspection over the threats women face in India, whether on the streets of the capital city or in the lanes of a distant village, despite the advances of India's liberalizing society and invigorated economy. Her life embodied the modern Indian dream, the one-generation upward transformation that millions are pursuing.

The Wall Street Journal reconstructed the details of her life from interviews with family and friends, including the young man, a 28-year-old software engineer, who was with her when she was beaten. He was treated and released but still requires medical attention. The *Journal* is refraining from publishing the woman's name, in keeping with Indian laws governing the identification of rape victims.

The young woman, the child of an airport laborer who earns 7,000 rupees a month (about $130), was determined, her friends and family said, to become the first from her family, which hails from a caste of agricultural workers, to have a professional career. She was on the cusp of achieving it. She had enrolled in a years-long physio-therapy course in a city in the foothills of the Himalayas. To afford it, she worked nights at an outsourcing firm, helping Canadians with their mortgage issues, said family members and her friend.

As she amassed some money of her own, she enjoyed figuring out how to spend it. Lately, she had her eye on a Samsung smartphone. One day she hoped to buy an Audi. "I want to build a big house, buy a car, go abroad and will work there," her friend, the software engineer, recalled her saying.

On January 7, the five men who allegedly raped and killed her appeared before a Delhi court for the first time, their faces covered in gray woolen caps. All five face charges of kidnapping, rape and murder, among other crimes. They face the death sentence if found guilty. A sixth alleged assailant, a juvenile, will face proceedings before a juvenile court.

A lawyer for the accused couldn't be reached.

The family originally hails from Ballia, in rural Uttar Pradesh state. They moved to the capital city, Delhi, about 30 years ago to seek "a better life," Bitiya's father said. He worked for 13 years as a mechanic at an appliance fac-tory. Then he struggled for a decade in his own business, assembling voltage meters. He worked as a hospital secu-rity guard.

About three years ago, he became a loader at the air-port. He sold half of a small parcel of land to pay for the education of his daughter and her two younger brothers, who were 17 and 15 years old at the time.

The family lives in Mahavir Enclave, on a 6-foot-wide lane off a decrepit street lined with shoe shops, dispensaries and jewelry stores. It is a neighborhood of migrants who work as construction laborers, building apartment houses for Delhi's blossoming middle class.

Bitiya's brothers recalled pillow fights with their elder sister, who was only 5 foot 3 and weighed about 90 pounds. But she stood out as a high achiever in school. She earned pocket money tutoring other children. "She was the brightest student in the classroom," said a school friend who identified herself only as Nisha.

At first, Bitiya had wanted to be a doctor. But her father couldn't afford her tuition or find a suitable guarantor for a loan, which a bank would require.

The Sai Institute of Paramedical and Allied Sciences, in the city of Dehradun in the Himalayan foothills, offered an alternative: a four-and-a-half-year physiotherapy course that was more affordable. She enrolled in November 2008. A graduate from the school is expected to earn a monthly salary of nearly 30,000 rupees (about $550), more than four times what her father earns.

She attended classes from noon to 5:00 P.M., staff and her friends said. To pay the fees, she worked at a call center on the 7:00 P.M. to 4:00 A.M. shift, handling questions from Canadians about their mortgages and supervising a team of employees, friends and family said. The company couldn't be located.

When she first arrived at school in Dehradun, she was an "introverted and submissive" young woman who wore simple traditional dresses, said Bhawna Ghai, a professor and head of the physiotherapy department. But as the course progressed, she opened up. She left the dorm and moved into an apartment with two friends. She began choreographing and emceeing college dance recitals.

A good English speaker, she became an avid reader, particularly Sidney Sheldon novels, her college friends said. She was a fan, too, of *One Night @ the Call Center*, a bestselling novel by Indian author Chetan Bhagat about six call center workers.

Money remained an issue. Combining her studies and the call center job was exhausting, friends said. "She slept for only two hours" a night, said Sheen Kaur, one of her roommates, in an interview. In all, she paid the equivalent of about $3,300 in tuition fees.

Along the way, she developed an eye for fashion. If she spotted an outfit at the mall that she couldn't afford, her brother said, she would find ways to replicate it in the bazaars. She amassed a shoe collection, preferably high heels.

In October 2012, she returned to Delhi to look for a volunteer internship, a requirement to complete her physiotherapy studies.

On December 16, the day of the attack, her family gathered at their home. The young woman and her mother cooked lunch—fritters in yogurt, beans and puffy bread called *puri*. The siblings teased each other about who would steal a bite of their father's food.

After lunch, their father went to work on the 2:00 P.M. shift at the airport, one of her brothers recalled. And his sister went to see her friend at the mall, the meeting the two had earlier arranged on the phone. The two weren't dating, both he and the family said, but had been friends for years.

At the mall, her friend recalled noticing that Bitiya had put streaks in her hair—white, gold and red. She asked him what he thought. He says he wasn't really a fan of the look, but answered, "It's okay," so as not to hurt her feelings. He also remarked that she seemed too thin.

"A lot of people struggle to get this physique," she responded.

After *Life of Pi* ended—she loved the movie, her friend said—they took a motorized rickshaw to Munirka, on Delhi's main southern highway, a convenient point to board a bus toward her home.

The same evening, about five miles away, in a slum of about 300 dwellings known as Ravi Dass Camp, two brothers, Ram and Mukesh Singh, were throwing a small party with chicken and alcohol, according to police. Ram was the driver of a private bus.

They were joined that evening by Vinay Sharma, a young man who earned $40 a month as a helper at a local gym, police said. Earlier he had been watching television at home, according to his mother, Champa Devi, when a friend and local fruit seller, Pawan Gupta, stopped by. Eventually, according to police, the two men joined the Singh brothers, who lived down a narrow lane nearby.

The group, which included one other man and a juvenile, decided to take what police have described as a "joy ride" on the bus that Ram Singh drove.

Around 9:15 P.M., police said, the bus pulled into the stop where Bitiya and her friend were looking for a ride. The men aboard the bus offered them a lift to Dwarka, near the young woman's home, according to police.

Four of the alleged assailants acted like regular passengers, according to Bitiya's friend. One of them collected 20 cents for each ticket, and the other drove.

The accused began taunting Bitiya with lewd comments, according to her friend, which led to a brawl. Bitiya's friend said that some of the men knocked him unconscious with an iron bar.

At the back of the bus, police said, the young woman was raped as the vehicle was driven around, passing Vasant Vihar, an upscale neighborhood that is home to embassies and expatriates. After about 40 minutes, according to police, the bus stopped near a strip of budget neon-lit hotels with names such as Star, Venus and Highway Crown, which cater to travelers near the airport.

There, the men on the bus dumped the two friends, naked, by the side of the road on a dusty strip of dried grass, according to police and the young man. As the woman lay barely conscious, her friend, who was bleeding from a cut to the head but could now stand, waved his arms and shouted for help at passing cars. For more than 20 minutes, he said, no one stopped.

Several people who work in the area said that two employees of DSC Ltd., the company that built the highway and now runs it, were the first to attend to the two victims, around 10:00 P.M. One of the DSC employees put in a call to the police, according to a person familiar with the matter.

Moments later, a manager from one of the nearby hotels, a burly 28-year-old, got on his motorbike to head home. He passed the scene without stopping—but then turned back, struck by the image of blood streaming down the young man's face.

He offered to get a sheet and a bottle of water from his hotel to cover the two as they waited for the police, he said in an interview. One of the DSC employees gave a sweater to the young woman and a shirt to her friend. About 45 minutes after the two were dumped, the police arrived.

Around the same time as Bitiya was being taken by police to Safdarjung Hospital, about eight miles away, her family was starting to grow concerned. Usually, her brother said, Bitiya returned home by 8:30 P.M. "We were really worried, but didn't have any other option than waiting," he said. He dialed the pair's mobile phones without success.

Around 11:15 P.M., the police phoned and said the young woman had been in an accident. Her father rushed to the hospital with a neighbor on a motorbike. "It was a sinking feeling," her brother said. "We feared for the worst."

—*Preetika Rana, Amol Sharma and Aditi Malhotra in Delhi contributed to this article.*

2

A Love Story

BY KRISHNA POKHAREL

She called him "a perfect man." He still keeps her number stored in his cell phone, under the name Jewi, derived from a Sanskrit word meaning "life."

"She was the closest person to my heart," says the young man. Soon he is expected to tell a judge about the night she was raped aboard a private bus here, an attack that left his friend dead and the world horrified.

"I find myself surrounded by the pictures in my mind of the incident of that night in the bus," says the 28-year-old information technology specialist, who was himself badly injured in the December 16 attack. Broad-chested and plainspoken, he now walks with a cane.

Speaking with *The Wall Street Journal*, he gave new details of the assault and described his close and complex relationship with Bitiya, a petite recent college graduate who was 23 at the time of her death.

The case has stirred widespread protest and calls for justice. Five men face charges including rape, kidnapping and murder. Lawyers for the five say they are innocent. A sixth person accused, a juvenile, faces proceedings in juvenile court. A lawyer representing him couldn't be reached.

In many ways, the young man and his friend were a modern dating couple, yet still bound by caste and tradition. Living away from home, the two were making their way in India's widening professional class—she was a physiotherapist looking for her first job; he leads a team specializing in Internet voice technology for corporations.

They shared their problems, took vacations together and consulted each other even over the purchase of a pair of shoes. She once talked him out of investing in a company that turned out to be a fraud. He gave her the log-in details to his Facebook account.

Their families were aware of their closeness and didn't interfere, the young man and her family said. But the two friends felt their relationship would always be a friendship and not a marriage, he says. He came from a high-caste Brahmin background. His father is a prominent lawyer. His family lives in a three-story home with servants' quarters.

By contrast, Bitiya hailed from a Kurmi agrarian caste that is lower on the Hindu hierarchy. Her family lives in a small concrete-and-brick house near the Delhi airport, where her father works as a baggage handler.

Differences like these worked against a union. And the young man says he was loath to go against his family's strong wishes that he find a traditional match from within his Brahmin community.

"We just didn't talk about it because it would sour our relationship," he says of his friend. "We were of equal status as friends."

In an interview, the young woman's mother said to the question of marriage, "You can't really say what could have happened in the future."

The young man's father says the subject of marriage never came up, but had their son made a fervent case, the family "might have given it a thought."

The two first made contact in December 2010. It wasn't exactly a success. A mutual friend had suggested that the young man help her with her studies, and gave her his number.

Hi, how are you? she texted him. what's going on?

He thought it was the mutual friend playing a prank.

I know who you are, man, he replied. is this your new number?

I am not a boy, i am a girl, she responded.

The mutual friend intervened to end the confusion. Two months later, when the young woman was visiting Delhi from her college in Dehradun, about five hours' drive away, he went to meet her for the first time at the bus station.

He guessed who she was. She was wearing a red top, a blue skirt and high heels, he says.

By way of breaking the ice, he walked up and asked, "Where do I get a bus to Dehradun?"

Without even looking up, she pointed away. So he had to introduce himself.

Over lunch at McDonald's and an afternoon tour of Delhi's ancient Red Fort, they started getting to know each other. "I told her that I am from Gorakhpur," a city in northern India, he says, recalling that day. "That I am from a Brahmin family. I have two brothers and three sisters. I am very close to my mother. That my father is a lawyer. That I worship God daily. That I am a foodie and like to go for movies. I drink milk daily. I am fond of wristwatches and have a good collection of them."

It would grow into a welcome friendship as he found his way in Delhi, where he moved in 2006 after graduating in engineering from a technical college. Back home in Gorakhpur, he had founded a group that he intended to focus on women's empowerment and child development. But his family advised him to "first prove yourself, then work for others," he says.

He joined his current employer in 2008. "He is a professionally very efficient person, a quiet worker, very responsible and hardworking," says his boss there.

As the friendship grew, he and the young woman spoke frequently on the phone. "She was that friend for me with whom I can talk about my financial status and family problems openly," he says. At times, he says, she called him "a perfect man."

They started taking trips together to see holy sites. On May 10, 2011, her birthday, they met in Haridwar, a Hindu pilgrimage center on the Ganga River, about an hour's drive from where she studied.

They traveled on cable cars to hillside temples before watching devotees take evening dips and worship the river.

By then, her family knew and liked him. He was the friend she spoke to most, her mother says. "We thought of him as a gentleman," she says. "He was safe."

Five months later, the couple visited Vaishno Devi, another popular pilgrimage spot in the Himalayas. "It was very cold. We took the Shalimar Express train from Dehradun," he says.

They climbed about seven miles to the sanctuary, worshiped there that evening, and hiked back to the hotel the following morning. "We bought some medicines for our legs that were aching severely," he says, smiling sheepishly at the memory. "She also provided some physiotherapy treatment to my legs," he said, pantomiming a rub on his leg.

In March, they went together to a shrine devoted to the Indian spiritual guru Sai Baba, in the state of Maharashtra. A few months later, he gave her some inspirational books when they traveled to Rishikesh, another Hindu holy site famously visited by the Beatles in 1968.

Her last gift to him was a gray tie. It remains in an envelope in his Delhi apartment. "I tried to do things that made her happy," he says. "It's because that's how I could be happy, too."

On their trips, they would share a hotel room. They held hands and hugged, he says, but didn't go further. "Regarding the man-woman relationship, I have conservative views," he says. They sang, joked and played cards and chess. He thought about her often when they were apart.

When they met on December 16, the day of the attack, the two hadn't seen each other for several weeks. "It was a strange and boring day," he says.

That evening, after watching *Life of Pi* at a mall, they strolled by a fountain and snapped some pictures. He wanted to linger, but she was eager to get home, he says.

They hailed a motorized rickshaw to a bus stop where she could catch a ride home. A bus was there waiting, and someone on board called out to them, "Didi, where do you have to go?" (*Didi* means "elder sister.") The person calling out was the juvenile defendant later accused in the crime, the young man says.

The young man says the two boarded the bus and sat in the second row. The row in front was occupied by two men who appeared to be passengers, as did two other men seated across the aisle, he says.

Things were normal for about five minutes, he says, and he began to relax. "It's okay for today," he says he told Bitiya, "but don't board these kinds of buses in the future."

Then three of the men asked the couple what they were doing with each other out at night, he says. That is when he knew they were in trouble.

He and his friend started shouting. She tried to call the police, but one of the men snatched her phone away, he says. He got into a struggle with one of the men. He says he heard shouts of "Bring the rod, bring the rod!"

He was struck repeatedly on the back of the head and pounded on his legs, he says. Dizzy and bleeding, he fell to the floor. Police have accused the assailants of using a metal rod from the bus's luggage rack in the assault.

Bitiya was dragged to the back of the bus, he says. The lights were off. He heard her crying for help, but he was pinned to the floor by one or more men, he says. Police allege Bitiya was gang-raped and sexually assaulted with a metal rod.

"I go to that moment again and again," the young man says. "Just an hour before, everything was fine, and all of a sudden, everything had gone horribly wrong."

Finally, he says, he heard the words "She's dead, she's dead."

The couple was thrown off the bus at the side of a highway, according to the young man and the police. The two had been stripped naked. Bitiya was still alive. Eventually, they were brought to a hospital.

A lawyer for the driver of the bus has said his client acknowledged that a rape happened on his bus, but that he is innocent of all the charges. A lawyer for two of the accused has said his clients weren't on the bus at the time of the incident. A lawyer for another of the accused has said his client was tortured into making a false confession; police have declined to comment on that allegation. That lawyer has requested that the trial be moved outside Delhi, arguing that his client won't get an impartial hearing locally. The Indian Supreme Court dismissed that request. A lawyer for the fifth accused has said his client is innocent, too.

The father of the dead young woman, speaking of her friend's efforts on the night of the attack, says, "We are eternally thankful to him." If he hadn't been there, he says, his daughter might have disappeared without a trace.

Five days later, the young man visited his friend in the intensive care unit of Delhi's Safdarjung Hospital. She had been so violently raped and beaten that much of her intestines had to be surgically removed.

He says he apologized to her for letting her down. She replied, if only we had stayed longer by the fountain at the mall, as you wished, perhaps we would have missed the bus.

She reminded him that it was exactly two years since they had first texted, he says. She tried to hug him but she couldn't get up because of the medical equipment attached to her body. "She made a gesture of a hug," he says.

Later, she was transferred to Singapore for treatment. The young man says he learned of her death from a television report.

Today, he says, he weighs what might have been between the two of them. "I would have been with her all my life," he said in one interview. "Even if that meant taking the extreme step of going against the wishes of my family."

—*Saurabh Chaturvedi contributed to this article.*

3

The Suspects

BY AMOL SHARMA, VIBHUTI AGARWAL AND ADITI MALHOTRA

Vinay Sharma, a gym assistant who prided himself on his six-pack abs, arrived home late the evening of December 16, his mother said. As he ate dinner, she asked him where he had been.

"Around," he told his mother, Champa Devi.

Then he went to bed in the family's tiny slum home. Two days later, a policeman knocked on the door.

Mr. Sharma now faces murder charges in the events of December 16—the night the young physiotherapy student was so brutally raped aboard a bus here, in India's capital, that she ultimately died of her injuries. The death has inspired soul-searching across India to understand the violence of the act.

Mr. Sharma, police say, was one of a group of six on a bus that set out "to pick up a female passenger and to have sex and make merry," according to a police document reviewed by *The Wall Street Journal*. The document sheds new light on the details of the evening's alleged events.

Five men have been charged with rape, murder, kidnapping and other offenses. The sixth is a juvenile runaway, someone who was popular as a helper on buses because he was skillful at attracting fares in a "singsong way," a police report says. He is expected to face proceedings in juvenile court.

A lawyer for Mr. Sharma, along with lawyers for two others, denies that their clients were on the bus that night and said they were innocent of all charges.

To reconstruct the lives of the men and the events of the evening of December 16, the *Journal* interviewed family members, friends and lawyers for the accused. Like the dead young woman—who had roots in a dirt-poor village but was poised to make the leap into a well-paying medical career—several of the men were from families that had moved to the big city to improve their lot as India's economy flourished. Their lives, however, followed a different arc.

None had managed to seize opportunity. Mr. Sharma earned about $54 a month, his mother said, in a gym that had been one of the venues for the 2010 Commonwealth Games. The evening of the alleged attack, she said, he had borrowed 20 cents to top up the minutes on his mobile phone.

Akshay Kumar, another of the accused, is the youngest of three sons of a small-time farmer in Bihar—one of India's most impoverished states—according to relatives. He left school after the seventh grade and in 2010 married Punita Devi; they have a young son, Ms. Devi said in a telephone interview from their village.

Mr. Kumar, 24 years old, moved to Delhi last summer, his wife said. At a bus repair shop, he befriended a driver named Ram Singh, according to Mr. Kumar's brother, and began working on Mr. Singh's bus so he could learn to drive.

His lawyer denied Mr. Kumar was on the bus at the time of the attack and said he was innocent.

Mr. Singh, 33 years old, is one of the accused, along with his brother, 22-year-old Mukesh. Both are drivers. Before that, they worked as day laborers building roads and houses, said a relative and neighbor, Asha, who uses only one name.

A lawyer for Mukesh Singh said his client wasn't on the bus and is innocent. He said his client had been tortured by police. The police declined to comment.

V. K. Anand, the lawyer representing Ram Singh, said that, in an interview with his client, Ram Singh acknowledged he had been drinking that night and that a rape occurred on the bus.

About 50 yards from where Ram and Mukesh Singh live is the house of Mr. Sharma, the gym assistant. His parents grew up in villages in Uttar Pradesh, where their families farmed wheat and chickpeas. They moved to Delhi about 20 years ago.

Mr. Sharma's father first worked as a balloon seller on a bicycle. Recently, he worked in construction at Delhi's airport, making about $90 a month.

"I thought that coming here would be an opportunity to educate my children so that they can do well in life," said Ms. Devi, Mr. Sharma's mother.

Unlike many children in the neighborhood, Mr. Sharma, who police say is 20, completed his schooling. He speaks decent English and had a habit of asking people how they got ahead so he could follow in their footsteps, his mother said. "I wanted him to be able to support us when we grew old."

A keen bodybuilder, Mr. Sharma took protein supplements and watched his diet, avoiding rice because of the calories. He spent his free time watching cartoons and playing marbles with his 13-year-old brother, his mother said, or helping him with his homework.

On the evening of December 16, Mr. Sharma was watching TV when his friend from down the lane, fruit seller Pawan Gupta, stopped by to ask him to go for a walk, his mother said. As the two men walked, they were hailed from the bus that Ram Singh drove, according to Ms. Devi. Her younger son witnessed it as he played marbles, she said.

The men boarded along with several children, according to Ms. Devi's account. The children later disembarked, she said. Mr. Sharma and Mr. Gupta stayed on, according to police.

Also on the bus, police say, were Ram and Mukesh Singh, Mr. Kumar, and the runaway boy with the singsong voice. The Singh brothers had been drinking before they took the bus out, police say.

Around 9:15 P.M., the bus picked up two passengers, the 23-year-old young woman and her friend, as they made their way home after watching a movie at a mall, police say. The men beat the male friend, according to police, and raped the woman. Both victims were assaulted with a metal rod before they were dumped, naked, on the side of a highway, where they were picked up and taken to a hospital, according to police.

The police document cites a medical report that the young woman was slapped in the face, kicked in the abdomen, and bitten on the lips, cheek, breast and elsewhere in an assault that lasted 30 minutes. A police spokesman declined to comment. The woman required surgery to her intestines. She was flown for treatment to Singapore, where she died December 29.

The police document also cites a confession that it says was made by Ram Singh. In it, he said, he and the others washed the bus after the attack, removing flesh from the seats, according to the document. They burned the victims' clothes, the document said.

Mr. Anand, the lawyer representing Ram Singh, said he didn't dispute that his client made a statement to police but said it wasn't, under Indian law, admissible as evidence in court. A lawyer for the fifth accused, Pawan Gupta, couldn't be reached.

On December 17, police say, they found Ram Singh on the bus and took him into custody. The green-and-black

T-shirt and the plastic sandals he was wearing were blood-stained, according to the police document. Mr. Anand, Ram Singh's lawyer, said the allegations in the document "are not sufficient evidence to convict Ram Singh."

Over the next few days, the police in Delhi detained Mukesh Singh, Mr. Gupta and the juvenile. Mr. Kumar was apprehended by police in his village in Bihar. Police have recovered the young woman's Nokia mobile phone and her friend's shoes, the police document said.

Two days after the attack, Mr. Sharma, the gym assistant, was awakened from a nap by a knock on the door, his mother said. "Namaste, are you Vinay Sharma?" said the policeman, using a Hindi greeting. "Please come outside with me."

—Saptarishi Dutta, Rajesh Roy, Preetika Rana and Tripti Lahiri contributed to this article.

4

The Family

BY SAURABH CHATURVEDI

The brutal gang rape of a 23-year-old physiotherapy student in December sparked global attention and monetary compensation for her family, but family members say the gestures haven't helped soften the blow of their loss.

The attack, which took place on a moving bus in India's capital, sparked intense pressure for the government to take action to combat widespread sexual assault.

U.S. Secretary of State John Kerry honored the victim with a U.S. government award given to courageous women around the world in recognition of her bravery in recording police statements about the rape before she died at a Singapore hospital at the end of December.

The attack also led to an outpouring of sympathy for the victim's parents, poor migrants from the northern state of Uttar Pradesh who, like many Indians, put up with financial hardships in the hope of a better life for their children.

Three state governments, including Delhi's, have given the family around $90,000 in compensation—a large sum for a family whose father earns $130 a month as a baggage handler at Delhi's international airport.

The parents and the victim's two younger brothers soon will be moving from their modest concrete-and-brick house on the outskirts of Delhi to a modern government apartment—another gift from authorities. The central government has offered the elder son a state job or to pay for his college tuition.

Others have promised to help. The college in the northern city of Dehradun where the woman studied says it will soon refund $3,000 in fees to the family and has offered free education to her brothers. Yuvraj Singh, who plays for India's national cricket team, says he is planning to visit the family soon to offer them $3,000, the amount he won in December for being named the best player in an international match against England.

The victim's parents, in a recent interview at their Delhi home, appeared ambivalent about the attention they are receiving.

"We feel the deepest of pains when we spend the compensation money," the mother said. "[Bitiya] was putting in all the effort for a better life, for more money and a better place to live in. Now we have the money but we don't have her."

Facing public pressure, India's government in February proposed legislative changes that would increase the maximum punishment for convicted rapists to the death penalty from life imprisonment and widen the definition of sexual assault. The proposed changes need to be approved by Parliament.

Human rights groups criticized the government for attacking the problem with the death penalty. Women's groups say other measures, such as punishing police officers who refuse to take action on a rape complaint and speeding up court procedures against rapists, would be more effective. There are as many as 100,000 rape cases pending in India's legal system, activists estimate.

But the victim's parents say they want their daughter's killers to die. Five men have been charged with her murder. They could face the death penalty if found guilty, as Indian law sanctions capital punishment for murder. They have entered not guilty pleas. The case of a sixth person, who is under 18 years old, is being heard in juvenile court for his alleged role in the gang rape. If found to have participated, he faces up to three years in jail. He has pleaded not guilty.

"We want the culprits to be hanged," the victim's father said.

The mother says she spends her days crying, doing household chores and flipping through news channels to get updates on the trials. The victim's elder brother, a high school graduate who is 17, has stopped preparing for exams in April to get into engineering college, where he hopes to pursue an undergraduate degree.

"For whom should we do it now? For whom should I study and for whom should we do good with our lives? We have lost all the motivation and interest," the elder brother said.

His 15-year-old brother is taking high school exams this month, but says he is unable to concentrate. He says he can't stop thinking about the new phone the brothers had planned to buy their sister as a birthday present in May to replace her battered handset.

The father, who is in his mid-50s, has been unable to resume work at the airport for the past two months because of a knee infection. He worries that, despite the compensation, the family will again fall on hard times unless he or his sons can find better-paid employment. But he refuses to give up hope of a return to normalcy.

"If you think why, what and for whom to do anything now, then you have already lost the plot. If there's a will, there are many ways," he said.

The mother recently packed her daughter's clothes into a bag and locked it in the room where she stayed on breaks from studies in Dehradun. She regrets being unable to say good-bye properly to her daughter.

"She never thought that she was dying," the mother said. "She didn't say, 'In my absence, please do this, please do that.' So generally we couldn't really have the last talk where we could really pour our hearts out."

5

Death in Prison

BY VIBHUTI AGARWAL AND PREETIKA RANA

One of the five men accused in the gang rape of a 23-year-old Indian woman—a crime that received widespread international attention—was found dead in jail, his lawyer said on Monday, March 11.

Ram Singh was found dead at Tihar Jail, Delhi's main prison, at around 5:15 A.M., said his lawyer, V. K. Anand.

Mr. Singh, 33 years old, and four other men were being held at the jail during their trial at a special court in Delhi on charges that include kidnapping, rape and murder. The five men have pleaded not guilty.

"He hanged himself [from] the ceiling with his own clothes," said Sunil Gupta, spokesman for Tihar Jail.

Mr. Gupta said Mr. Singh had three cellmates. He said the cellmates "were clueless about his intention to commit suicide. They were sleeping when the incident happened."

V. K. Anand spoke with the media at the Delhi hospital where Mr. Singh's body was later taken for autopsy.

Rajinder Singh, Delhi's assistant commissioner of police, who is part of a special task force investigating the Delhi rape case, said Mr. Singh used his "own clothes" to hang himself.

"He used the sleeping mat to make a noose, string from his trousers as a rope to hang himself."

Mr. Singh's lawyer contested the police version.

"It is not possible he committed suicide. And the theory that he used his own clothes can't be true as there is high security inside the prison," Mr. Anand said.

Mr. Gupta denied allegations of negligence by jail authorities. "I am aware media channels are accusing jail authorities for negligence, but I deny this allegation. There are guards outside every ward here in Tihar. Ram Singh's ward, too, had sufficient guards. It is not possible to have guards outside" every cell, he said.

Mr. Gupta said the four other accused men at Tihar, who are in neighboring cells, are being closely watched by jail authorities following the suicide.

Addressing reporters in Delhi, Indian home minister Sushil Kumar Shinde said, "It's a major lapse. It's not a small incident. It's a suicide."

"A magisterial inquiry has been ordered. Things will be clear once the report comes," he added.

The five men, along with a juvenile who faces juvenile court proceedings, are accused of luring the young woman and a male friend onto a bus, then beating the friend and beating and sexually assaulting the woman with a metal rod before throwing both of them naked onto the side of a highway on the evening of December 16.

The young woman, a physiotherapy student, later died of her injuries. Mr. Singh was the regular driver of the bus, one of thousands of private buses that ply the capital's streets.

The case drew widespread attention in India and worldwide for its brutality and for the spotlight it shone on India's failure to protect women. The bus traveled around South Delhi, near an enclave popular with diplomats, for about 45 minutes as the assault took place. Protesters marched in Delhi and other Indian cities, and the government has since moved to strengthen laws to deter crimes against women.

Assistant commissioner of police Rajinder Singh said Mr. Singh's body had been moved to a nearby hospital for a postmortem. "Only after the inquiry is done by special district magistrate, we can say what exactly happened," he said.

Reached by telephone, the father of the rape victim said, "We are feeling a bit relieved with this development. But we really don't know what more to say right now."

Mr. Anand said that during the last court hearing, on March 8, Mr. Singh "looked cheerful since he met his 5-year-old son in the court." He said he didn't know what had driven Mr. Singh to this extreme step. "He was happy with the way the trial was proceeding."

A. P. Singh, a lawyer for Akshay Kumar and Vinay Sharma, two others facing trial, said he was skeptical about authorities' explanation that Mr. Singh hanged himself. "How is it possible for a prisoner to hang himself inside a jail cell? Is Tihar's security so weak?"

He added, "My clients are terrified, scared, they fear for their safety."

Mr. Singh's father said in an interview that the family, too, doubted the official version of events. "I had met him six days back," said Mange Lal. "He said the authorities are not treating him well." He also noted that Mr. Singh couldn't use one of his hands efficiently since an accident several years ago.

Tihar's spokesman has said the prisoners in the rape case have been treated properly and confirmed that authorities believe it was a suicide.

—*Saurabh Chaturvedi, Rajesh Roy, R. Jai Krishna and
Aditi Malhotra contributed to this article.*

6

Climate of Fear

BY AMOL SHARMA, BIMAN MUKHERJI AND RUPA SUBRAMANYA

*B*ARASAT, *India*—Juhi Nondi, a 20-year-old college student, takes the train every day to and from school here, toting a satchel of textbooks and looking stylish in her skinny jeans and T-shirts—and long, sharp fingernails.

"They're not just for fashion," she says of her pink nails, "but also for self-defense."

Aggressive sexual harassment is a daily part of her commute in this bustling suburb of Kolkata. A man grabbed her breast one morning, she says. Another day, someone grabbed her hip. Friends carry chili powder, she says, to throw in the eyes of an assailant, a sort of home-made pepper spray.

"If I'm even a half hour late coming home, my parents panic," Ms. Nondi says.

Barasat, which boasts a shopping mall, a KFC restaurant and a growing number of women in the workplace, is a typical if modest Indian economic success story. But it is typical of urban India in another way, too: here and nationwide, women say harassment of women is a fixture of daily life.

In December, India's climate of sexual violence burst onto the world's consciousness after a young woman on a bus in Delhi was so brutally gang-raped and assaulted that she died of her injuries. That attack provoked nationwide protests and prompted national introspection about the broader spectrum of harassment, from stalking to groping, that often goes unpunished and can lead to more aggravated assault, experts say.

Here in Barasat, interviews with two dozen women yielded consistent stories of recent and repeated harassment. Men trail women on foot or on scooters, making crude remarks and grabbing at the scarf worn to cover the chest. It happens at the train station, the women said, in the fish market lane, on the road to the university and outside the police station.

Many women interviewed complained that police do little to stop it. One local officer, when asked about this by a reporter, responded, "If these incidents don't happen, what will happen to our jobs?"

A senior Barasat police official said the police take all complaints seriously. The police said the department couldn't provide hard numbers on harassment complaints, arrests or convictions.

Women say they travel in groups, some carrying sharp objects (safety pins, pocketknives) to discourage harassers. Still, occasionally there are more serious assaults. In early 2011, a 16-year-old boy was stabbed to death trying to protect his 22-year-old sister, Rinku Das, as she returned home one evening from her call center job.

As usual, her brother picked her up on his bicycle from the station that day, Ms. Das says. Three men blocked the bike, she says, poured alcohol on her, and attacked her brother as he sprang to her defense.

As her brother was being beaten with bamboo canes, Ms. Das says, she pounded on a nearby senior police officer's bungalow. The guards outside told her they couldn't help. "I screamed and shouted for help in the middle of the street," she says.

Kalyan Banerjee, the main police officer dealing with Ms. Das's case, said the bungalow guards aren't allowed to leave their posts.

The three alleged attackers face murder charges and have pleaded not guilty. They are in judicial custody.

After the killing, police say, they intensified patrols, put more plainclothes officers on the street and opened a new women's police station, across from the Barasat Government College. From there, 18 female officers patrol high-frequency harassment areas.

But the roots of the problem run deep, starting in childhood. Across India, daughters are often less valued than sons, a reality that shows up in India's skewed gender ratios.

India has 37 million more men than women, partly because the preference for sons prompts sex-selective abortions and infanticide. Women also have a higher overall mortality rate than men, partly because of bias and neglect over a lifetime, according to recent research, as well as mortality during childbirth.

Some argue that the harassment is a byproduct of economic growth in places such as Barasat. A few decades ago, Barasat was a dirt-road town of a few thousand people. Today it is a growing suburb of sprawling Kolkata, with apartment buildings and gated communities with names such as Fortune Township. The population tops a quarter million.

Men and women alike have benefited greatly, but society remains deeply conservative. "For generations, men haven't seen women so empowered," says Mayank Saksena, an executive at consulting firm Jones Lang LaSalle who has developed real estate in Barasat and has studied the town closely. "It builds jealousy and envy."

In particular, men lacking enough formal education to climb the economic ladder may find casual work as food vendors, rickshaw pullers, drivers or laborers, which might pay about $100 per month. Around them, in Barasat, they see growing numbers of young, modern women making their way to colleges and call centers.

A report commissioned by the Indian government after the Delhi rape and murder described the danger nationwide of "young, prospect-less men" whose frustrations are "lending intensity to a pre-existing culture of sexual violence."

In response to that report, the government has enacted a temporary ordinance that cracks down on various types of sexual harassment and assault. For example, "unwelcome and explicit sexual overtures" are punishable by up to five years in prison, while "making sexually coloured remarks" can yield a one-year jail term. Parliament must ratify the ordinance to make it permanent, otherwise it will expire in several weeks.

Anima Sarkar, a political science student, described an encounter with three Barasat men late last year. The 23-year-old and three of her male friends were walking the few hundred yards from the college to the train station when the men started verbally harassing her, she says. "Women are like a commodity, a product," she recalled one of them saying. "You are a good product."

She scolded one of them, she says, by asking, "Don't you have a sister or mother at home?"

A skirmish ensued between the men and Ms. Sarkar's friends. One man grabbed her scarf and hand, she says, and she slapped him.

Bystanders intervened and dragged one of the alleged attackers, Tapan Sen, down the street to the police station. Police later tracked down two other suspects, Mintu Sarkar (no relation to Anima) and Raju Biswas.

The men, who spent a night in jail, are out on bail as police investigate harassment-related charges. None has been charged with any wrongdoing. In interviews, they say they were out shopping that night and encountered Ms. Sarkar, but deny harassing or assaulting her.

They allege that a fourth man, whom they know by the nickname the Master, insulted and groped her.

Mr. Sen, 23, is a part-time driver who dropped out of school after ninth grade to work at a car repair shop. He earns about $75 a month.

Mr. Sarkar, 34 years old, owns a shop that makes door and window frames. "I really began this business from scratch," he said. He is unmarried and lives with his parents, two elder brothers and their wives. He has a high school diploma.

Mr. Biswas is a 23-year-old orphan with a wife, a 3-year-old daughter and no formal education. He says he makes about $150 a month as a contract laborer in Mr. Sarkar's shop, getting paid according to the number of pieces he makes.

The men described the fourth man, the Master, as a middle-aged part-time teacher who hung around their window-and-door-making shop. "He would stare lewdly at women passing by in the market," Mr. Biswas said.

According to Mr. Biswas's account, the Master was with them the night of the attack. He spoke to Ms. Sarkar and lunged at her, but then disappeared into the crowd, Mr. Biswas alleges, leaving the others to take the blame.

The Master couldn't be reached for comment. Police said they were unaware of him and his alleged role in the attack.

After the incident, Ms. Sarkar says, her neighbors told her parents that she must have done something wrong— that somehow the attack was her fault. Her parents grounded her for weeks, so she lost her job tutoring kids in math and science.

Ms. Sarkar, the daughter of a fruit vendor whose family of four lives on about $100 a month, plans to go to law school, but not in Barasat. "My friends and I say it's better if we run away from here when we graduate," she says.

Police say they are investigating charges of harassing a woman with intent to "outrage her modesty." Before the new ordinance, it was the only crime in India's criminal code dealing with harassment of women.

The law allows for a maximum of two years' imprisonment. In practice, such punishments are rare. Maheshwar Banerjee, public prosecutor in Barasat, said that since he took charge of the office in October 2011, he can't recall any harassment case that resulted in punishment.

Often the complainants don't appear in court because they are afraid of tarnishing their families' image or hurting their own marriage prospects, he said. "The women's families don't like to pursue the cases," he said.

The areas where women complain that harassment is most commonplace are the busy markets and intersections near the train station and in the heart of town. One lane leading from the station passes by the local courthouse. The other lane begins at a police station, passes a fish market and vegetable vendors, and reaches the office of the district magistrate, the most senior official.

The streets are packed with bicycle rickshaws and shoppers visiting jewelry stores, Internet cafés and snack vendors. Men gather at the tea stall on the road to the college.

Behind the college is an alley known for illegal liquor shops, where men drink and gamble. Barasat has one police officer for every 1,030 people (just about India's average), compared with one policeman per 390 people in the United States and one per 236 people in New York City.

Some policemen appear more concerned about being punished for not stopping harassment than about protecting women from such incidents, according to several women interviewed who commute regularly by train.

Shumi Kundu, 22, says that last month she had an encounter with two police officers who that left her with the impression they were more concerned about their own well-being than hers. At the time, she was sitting on a bench on a train platform. The cops approached her and asked her to leave.

"They said if I didn't leave and something bad happened to me, they'd be blamed for it," Ms. Kundu said.

A. K. Sarkar, an official in the Barasat Railway Police, which is in charge of security on train platforms, said officers take their duties seriously. "If anything at all happens, then we go and intervene," he said.

—*Uzma Jahangir contributed to this article.*

Epilogue

"Judge Sahib!"

On April 2, 2013, the Indian government enacted a new law that aims to improve the safety and security of the country's women. It was in direct response to the Delhi bus rape and the spotlight it put on the plight of India's women. The new law amends existing laws and criminal codes to provide harsher punishment against those convicted of crimes such as rape, stalking, voyeurism and throwing acid.

Local and international media have continued to report on more incidents of rape and attacks on women across India. In mid-March, a group of men allegedly gang-raped a 39-year-old Swiss tourist while she was camping with her husband in the central state of Madhya Pradesh. A few weeks later, public protests erupted again in Delhi when a 5-year-old girl was hospitalized with serious injuries after she was allegedly raped and assaulted by a man who lived in the same apartment block in East Delhi where she used to stay with her parents.

In the wake of the alleged rape of the 5-year-old, the office of Prime Minister Manmohan Singh issued a statement that said: "The Prime Minister has once again reiterated the need for society to look deep within and work to root out the evil of rape and other such crimes from our midst."

◆

At the end of May, the trial against the four remaining adult suspects in the December 16 Delhi bus rape case was ongoing at a special fast-track courtroom established inside a district court complex in South Delhi. The four men, who are in jail, have been charged with gang rape, kidnapping, murder and other crimes; each will face a maximum sentence of death if convicted. The lawyers for the prosecution and for the defendants said they expect the trial to be concluded and a verdict delivered by the end of July. A separate proceeding against the teenage suspect, who stays in a government-run shelter, is under way at Delhi's juvenile court. It's not clear when it will be completed.

◆

The male friend of Bitiya, the 23-year-old rape victim, has returned to work at the technology company where he has been employed since 2008 as a software engineer.

In the months following the incident, the company provided him paid leave for the treatment of his injuries and repeated appearances in the court as the main witness for the prosecution.

During weekends, he discusses with his friends his plans to revive the group that he had established at his home in Gorakhpur to work for the empowerment of women and the education of the children. "It pains me every time I read or hear about any new incident of rape and sexual attack," he says. "I feel that it's happening to me and my friend again."

On May 17, Bitiya's mother testified before a judge in the court where the four adult men are facing trial. Her testimony lasted for only about two minutes. "Judge sahib, give justice to my daughter!" she told the judge, addressing him with a local honorific.

Afterword

BY PAUL BECKETT AND KRISHNA POKHAREL

The state of women in the world's largest democracy has been given unprecedented attention since the Delhi gang rape in December 2012.

In the immediate aftermath of the incident, thousands of men and women took to the streets of Delhi and other cities to protest the lack of women's safety—and were met with tear gas and water cannons fired by police.

Faced with widespread outrage and international damage to India's image, the government has strengthened some laws to combat sexual assaults and has pledged to increase the number of women police officers to try to ensure that sexual assault cases are sensitively handled.

Women's organizations, civil-society groups and millions of Indians, male and female, are fighting to improve the situation of women in general. More crimes against women are being reported to police that may have been hushed up in the past.

But 21st-century India remains a paradox: a rapidly modernizing country in some respects but one with attitudes to the relationship between the sexes that are at odds with the notion of a vibrant participatory democracy of equal citizens—especially one that has several prominent women in its political leadership.

How India deals with this contradiction going forward will be vital to its growth—economic, political, cultural, demographic and social. A country cannot thrive when so many of its women feel intimidated when they participate in its development or are threatened when they try to assert their rights. Yet it will take a lot more than is presently being done to truly create a society of equals.

Reforming the laws is, in many ways, only a cosmetic solution. India already has a series of laws and other mechanisms in place designed to protect its women and its vulnerable citizens, such as the child welfare network that failed to rescue Baby Falak.

The problem is that existing laws are rarely enforced. India has a very low police-to-citizen ratio, its constables are poorly trained and meagerly paid, and its court system is clogged with cases. The government institutions that are supposed to anticipate and prevent crises are strapped for funds, rarely held accountable for failure, and rife with bureaucratic apathy.

Moreover, the momentum of outrage generated over women's safety after the Delhi rape already has waned. The pressure on politicians to enact meaningful reforms is receding in the run-up to the next general election. The drive for better governance has given way to rampant speculation over who will be picks for prime minister after elections are held by next spring.

Soon, the Delhi rape will likely occupy the same place in the social consciousness as the deaths of Baby Falak and Sister Valsa—incidents that attract attention, prompt calls for reforms, but ultimately become little more than newspaper shorthand for future tragedies.

What will it take to change this dynamic?

First, a genuine deterrent for perpetrators of crimes against women will require a huge investment in more and better-trained police, more judges and more efficient courts. Now men can largely act with impunity, knowing that, even if they are caught and can't bribe their way free, chances are high that they will be granted bail and not have to face trial for years.

Second, accountability for public servants is needed. The reaction to the Delhi rape case from some politicians was astonishing in its insensitivity, and was met with gasps by the commentariat on India's vibrant 24-hour television news cycle. But the message that India will not accept such views will have teeth only if it is enforced at the ballot box. The upcoming election should give voters the chance to send the message, and to put other politicians on notice, that improving governance and ensuring basic services and protections are the fundamental expectations from anyone whose name appears on the ballot.

Third, and most important, however, a change is required in the culture itself. For all its aspirations and trappings of Western modernity, India remains a deeply conservative country, one in which women are viewed by many men, and by many families, as in the service of their husbands and in-laws.

Dowry—the payment of money or gifts by a bride's family to her husband's in return for marriage—has not been diminished by India's economic rise. Rather, the value of the gifts expected by the husband's family has increased. Not to pay dowry threatens to "shame" a woman and her family. A similar attitude prevails when women are raped: that they have been shamed and their honor besmirched because they have endured a violent assault. Domestic assaults on women, as happened to Falak's mother, are rarely punished, and in fact are often viewed as a husband's natural response to a wife's dereliction of duty.

To change this will require nothing more than a revolution in how Indians view the fundamental relationship between men and women.

It will take more women demanding their rights, and getting a willing hearing. It will take more women standing up to the chauvinism of many Indian men and being heard when they yell that they won't take it anymore. It will take more women walking on the streets and going out at night, not retreating behind the walls of their homes out of fear of what might happen if they venture outside. It will take families saying, "No more," when a relative assaults a family member or sexually abuses a girl in the household, crimes that are very rarely now reported to police. And it will take a new generation of men to adopt an attitude toward women that is respectful of their bodies and their equal standing in society.

This is a tall order in the giant tumult that is daily life on the subcontinent. But for India to be the country that its greatest advocates contend it can be, it is a change that must happen, and fast.

New Delhi, April 8, 2013

Acknowledgments

The authors wish to thank Alex Martin, Jesse Pesta and the page-one staff of *The Wall Street Journal*; Elyse Tanouye, Karen Pensiero, Jason Conti and Craig Linder at *The Wall Street Journal* in New York; Raaj Mangal Prasad, former chairman of the Delhi Child Welfare Committee; Preetika Rana, Diksha Sahni, Aditi Malhotra, Saptarishi Dutta and the *India Real Time* staff; Geeta Anand and Amol Sharma of *The Wall Street Journal*'s India bureau.

About the Authors

KRISHNA POKHAREL is a New Delhi–based reporter with *The Wall Street Journal*. A native of Kathmandu, Nepal, he joined the *Journal*'s South Asia bureau in September 2007 while pursuing journalism studies at the University of Delhi. He writes on social issues.

PAUL BECKETT is Asia Editor of *The Wall Street Journal*. From 2007 until April, he ran the *WSJ*'s South Asia bureau. Born and bred in Scotland, he joined Dow Jones & Co. in 1990. He has reported from New York, London, Mexico City, Washington and New Delhi.

Credits

Cover design by Tomaso Capuano
Cover photograph by Getty Images

About the Publisher

Australia
HarperCollins Publishers (Australia) Pty. Ltd.
25 Ryde Road (P.O. Box 321)
Pymble, NSW 2073, Australia
http://www.harpercollins.com.au

Canada
HarperCollins Canada
2 Bloor Street East - 20th Floor
Toronto, ON, M4W, 1A8, Canada
http://www.harpercollins.ca

New Zealand
HarperCollins Publishers (New Zealand) Limited
P.O. Box 1
Auckland, New Zealand
http://www.harpercollins.co.nz

United Kingdom
HarperCollins Publishers Ltd.
77-85 Fulham Palace Road
London, W6 8JB, UK
http://www.harpercollins.co.uk

United States
HarperCollins Publishers Inc.
10 East 53rd Street
New York, NY 10022
http://www.harpercollins.com